CAMBRIDGE LIBRARY COLLECTION

Books of enduring scholarly value

Travel and Exploration

The history of travel writing dates back to the Bible, Caesar, the Vikings and the Crusaders, and its many themes include war, trade, science and recreation. Explorers from Columbus to Cook charted lands not previously visited by Western travellers, and were followed by merchants, missionaries, and colonists, who wrote accounts of their experiences. The development of steam power in the nineteenth century provided opportunities for increasing numbers of 'ordinary' people to travel further, more economically, and more safely, and resulted in great enthusiasm for travel writing among the reading public. Works included in this series range from first-hand descriptions of previously unrecorded places, to literary accounts of the strange habits of foreigners, to examples of the burgeoning numbers of guidebooks produced to satisfy the needs of a new kind of traveller - the tourist.

The Convict King

James Francis Hogan (1855–1924) wrote several histories of Irish colonisation in Australia. His family emigrated to Melbourne in 1856 where he became a respected author. After returning to Britain in 1893 he was elected a Member of Parliament, and he later became Professor of Irish History at University College Cork. This book, first published in 1891, retells the extraordinary life of Jorgen Jorgenson (1780–1841), a Danish adventurer, accomplished fraudster, amateur playwright and freelance preacher, who once declared himself the ruler of Iceland and eventually became Constable of Van Diemen's Land (Tasmania). Working from Jorgenson's autobiography (originally printed in the *Van Diemen's Land Annual* 1835 and 1838), Hogan describes his early adventures as a sailor, his 'liberation' of Iceland from Denmark in 1809, his employment as a British spy, his imprisonment at Newgate and arrival in Tasmania as a convict, and his participation in the infamous Aboriginal clearances there.

Cambridge University Press has long been a pioneer in the reissuing of out-of-print titles from its own backlist, producing digital reprints of books that are still sought after by scholars and students but could not be reprinted economically using traditional technology. The Cambridge Library Collection extends this activity to a wider range of books which are still of importance to researchers and professionals, either for the source material they contain, or as landmarks in the history of their academic discipline.

Drawing from the world-renowned collections in the Cambridge University Library, and guided by the advice of experts in each subject area, Cambridge University Press is using state-of-the-art scanning machines in its own Printing House to capture the content of each book selected for inclusion. The files are processed to give a consistently clear, crisp image, and the books finished to the high quality standard for which the Press is recognised around the world. The latest print-on-demand technology ensures that the books will remain available indefinitely, and that orders for single or multiple copies can quickly be supplied.

The Cambridge Library Collection will bring back to life books of enduring scholarly value (including out-of-copyright works originally issued by other publishers) across a wide range of disciplines in the humanities and social sciences and in science and technology.

The Convict King

*Being the Life and Adventures
of Jorgen Jorgenson*

EDITED BY
JAMES FRANCIS HOGAN

CAMBRIDGE UNIVERSITY PRESS

Cambridge, New York, Melbourne, Madrid, Cape Town,
Singapore, São Paolo, Delhi, Tokyo, Mexico City

Published in the United States of America by Cambridge University Press, New York

www.cambridge.org
Information on this title: www.cambridge.org/9781108029667

© in this compilation Cambridge University Press 2011

This edition first published 1891
This digitally printed version 2011

ISBN 978-1-108-02966-7 Paperback

THE CONVICT KING.

" *Write* romances! Why, this poor old convict, Jorgen Jorgenson, who has been resting in his nameless grave these twenty years, has *lived* one beside which the ' story of Cambuscan bold,' the adventures of Gil Blas, or the doings of that prince of scoundrels, Mr. Barry Lyndon himself, dwindle into insignificance. All the raven-haired, hot-headed, supple-wristed soldiers of fortune that ever diced, drank, duelled, kissed, and escaladed their way through three volumes octavo, never had such an experience. Think over his story, from his birth in Denmark to his death in Van Diemen's Land, and imagine from what he *has* told us how much more he has been compelled to leave unrelated."

MARCUS CLARKE.

"JORGENSON IN CAPTIVITY."

(*From the original drawing by J. Jorgenson, in the Egerton Collection at the British Museum.*)

THE CONVICT KING.

THE LIFE AND ADVENTURES

OF

JORGEN JORGENSON

Monarch of Iceland, Naval Captain,
Revolutionist, British Diplomatic Agent, Author,
Dramatist, Preacher, Political Prisoner,
Gambler, Hospital Dispenser, Continental
Traveller, Explorer, Editor, Expatriated Exile,
and Colonial Constable.

RETOLD BY

JAMES FRANCIS HOGAN,

AUTHOR OF "The Irish in Australia," "The Australian in.
London," "The Lost Explorer," etc.

[With reproductions of Five Original Drawings by Jorgen Jorgenson
in the British Museum.]

WARD & DOWNEY
12, YORK STREET, COVENT GARDEN,
1891.

PRINTED BY
KELLY AND CO. LIMITED, GATE STREET, LINCOLN'S INN FIELDS,
AND KINGSTON-ON-THAMES.

ILLUSTRATIONS.

CONTENTS.

CHAPTER X.

CHAPTER XI.

APPENDIX A.

JORGENSON'S PUBLISHED WORKS.

APPENDIX B.

JORGENSON'S UNPUBLISHED REMAINS.

THE CONVICT KING.

THE CONVICT KING.

INTRODUCTION.

AMONGST the mass of commonplace offenders against her laws whom England banished to Botany Bay and Van Diemen's Land during the first half of the nineteenth century, were not a few remarkable characters of a superior type and with singular records; and the most conspicuous member of this class, the "usurping despot of a little reign," the only monarch who has left London for the Antipodes in a convict-ship, was the extraordinary adventurer whose chequered career is described in detail in the following pages. The name of Jorgen Jorgenson (Jürgensen is the strictly correct spelling) is not wholly unfamiliar to the reading public, for he has his little niche in all the biographical dictionaries; *

* See Cates' *Dictionary of General Biography*, page 670; Haydn, *Universal Index of Biography*, page 289; Maunder, *Biographical Treasury*, page 526; Ripley and Dana, *American Cyclopædia*, vol. 9, page 685; *Chambers' Encyclopædia*, vol. 5,

but these standard authorities abruptly dismiss him
on his transportation to Van Diemen's Land,
"where," they all agree in saying, "he is supposed
to have died shortly afterwards." * But this
gratuitous supposition is entirely erroneous. Jorgenson lived another active and adventurous career
extending over twenty years at the Antipodes—
he pushed himself to the front at both ends of
the earth — and wrote his autobiography in the
Van Diemen's Land Annual for 1835 and 1838.
This unique record of a strange, a kaleidoscopic, a
melo-dramatic life in real action I have thought

page 739; and Charles Knight's *English Cyclopædia*, vol. 3, page
652. For articles on Jorgenson in periodical literature consult
Household Words, vol. 14; *Edinburgh Review*, vol, 28; *Eclectic
Magazine*, vol. 57; *Colburn's Magazine*, vol. 126, and *Gentleman's
Magazine*, vol. 97. Incidental references to Jorgenson and his
career will be found in Sir W. J. Hooker's "Tour in Iceland;"
Sir G. MacKenzie's "Travels in Iceland," the Rev. S. Baring-
Gould's "Icelandic Scenes and Sagas," West and Fenton's histories
of Tasmania; Bonwick's "Last of the Tasmanians," Marcus
Clarke's "History of Australia," and David Blair's "History of
Australasia."

* All the biographical dictionaries and the cyclopædias erroneously
state that Jorgenson was transported to New South Wales. For
instance, *Knight's English Cyclopædia* says :—"Our impression
is that he died not long after his arrival in New South Wales, but
a search for a mention of the fact has proved unsuccessful." The
search was made in the wrong colony. It should have been
instituted in Van Diemen's Land.

worthy of being rescued from oblivion, and it will substantially be found in the following pages. I say substantially, because I have not made a literal transcript. Jorgenson was a foreigner, and notwithstanding his long residence in English lands and the considerable amount of practice he had both in speaking and writing our language, he never acquired a facility in English composition. Nearly all his numerous works are written in a style that is both unfamiliar and unattractive to the ordinary reader. I have therefore rewritten his autobiography, retaining all its characteristic features, adhering strictly to the recorded facts, but presenting them in what I trust will be found to be a readable and consecutive narrative. The original, it must be confessed, is rugged, unequal and discursive, but the inherent interest attaching to the autobiography of a daring adventurer whose life was so crowded with incident in both hemispheres, is amply sufficient to atone for all superficial imperfections. Jorgenson's authoritative history is now submitted for the first time to English readers, to whom it has hitherto been wholly unknown, buried as it has been for half a century in the dusty leaves of a long-defunct Antipodean periodical. It has been touched by only

1*

one hand during all that time. Some twenty years ago, my lamented friend, Marcus Clarke, the late eminent Australian novelist, discovered it in the course of his researches into the early convict life of the colonies, and made it the subject of an admirable essay in a Melbourne journal, the concluding paragraph of which I have quoted as the motto of this book.

Jorgenson's romantic and eventful career, the facts of which are attested by many independent and thoroughly trustworthy witnesses, is one of the most striking confirmations of the trite saying that truth is stranger than fiction. The most daring and unconventional of novelists would never dream of crowding into the life of a hero of the circulating libraries such a rapid succession of extraordinary adventures as actually befell this Anglo-Danish fortune-seeker in the nineteenth century. The apex of his adventurous career was reached when, through a combination of circumstances that he had never anticipated, he found himself elevated to the position of an autocrat in Iceland, the sovereign of a little Arctic kingdom. Excessive modesty was never one of his characteristics, yet he touches but comparatively lightly on this crowning episode in his autobiography, and therefore it may be well to supplement his narrative with some explanatory details of the Icelandic revolution from the recollections of trustworthy eye-witnesses. The most distinguished of these was the late Sir William Jackson Hooker, the eminent botanist and Director of the Royal Gardens at Kew. As a young man of twenty-four, enthusiastic in the study of his favourite science, and ambitious of making some original contributions to the world's knowledge of the flora and the natural wonders of Iceland, Sir William sailed with Jorgenson to the Arctic seas, and was a disinterested spectator of the series of events that culminated in his companion's assuming the authority of king of that northern island. In his "Tour of Iceland," published by Messrs. Longmans and John Murray in two volumes, Sir William embodied a complete, a graphic, and a thoroughly impartial account of the whole singular transaction.

By reason of its isolation and the severity of its climate, Iceland has at all times been under the necessity of drawing a large portion of its food supplies from the ports of its parent state, Denmark. Therefore it was that, during the war

between Great Britain and Denmark in 1809, the
unfortunate Icelanders were threatened with famine,
owing to the suspension of the customary supplies. In this emergency, Mr. Phelps, a leading
London merchant, saw an opportunity of combining
philanthropy and profit. He resolved to come to the
relief of the distressed Icelanders, and at the same
time to do some good business for himself. Accordingly he freighted the *Clarence* at Liverpool with
barley-meal, potatoes, salt, tobacco, sugar, coffee, etc.,
calculating on receiving in exchange a large and
valuable quantity of Icelandic produce, particularly
tallow. But, for the success of his enterprise, it was
necessary that somebody acquainted with the
Danish language, manners and customs, should go
out with the ship to act as intermediary and
facilitate trade. Jorgenson, who was then in
London on parole as a prisoner of war, offered
himself for this post and was accepted by Mr.
Phelps. At this time Jorgenson was only in his
twenty-eighth year, but he had already gone
through a succession of stirring experiences in
South Africa, Australia, Van Diemen's Land and
the Pacific Islands. He had acquired a thorough
knowledge of navigation in British ships, and when

he revisited his native Denmark after ten years'
absence, he was called upon to obey a decree commanding all Danes between the ages of eighteen
and fifty to serve their country in the war against
Great Britain. In pursuance of this decree, Jorgenson was appointed to the command of a
privateer of twenty-eight guns, called the *Admiral
Juul*, and off Flamborough Head he fell in with
the British man-of-war *Sappho*. An action of
forty-one minutes ensued and terminated in Jorgenson's defeat and the striking of his colours.
He was landed at Yarmouth, taken to London,
and liberated on parole. Such was his position when he started for Iceland as a representative of Mr. Phelps, without going through the
formality of asking the permission of the British
Government.

When the *Clarence* arrived at Iceland, such was
the anti-English hostility of the ruling Danish
powers, that she was at first refused permission to
land any portion of her cargo, notwithstanding the
dire straits to which many of the inhabitants were
reduced. But the people soon insisted on the
provisions being brought ashore, and the authorities
were reluctantly compelled to acquiesce. Having

landed his cargo and left an officer in charge to regulate its sale, Jorgenson brought the *Clarence* back to England, and a second expedition was then planned by Mr. Phelps, who was now so interested in the venture that he resolved to proceed to Iceland himself. The *Margaret and Anne,* a splendid ship carrying ten guns, was rapidly loaded, and sailed for Iceland with Mr. Phelps, Mr. (afterwards Sir William) Hooker, and Jorgenson on board. When they arrived, they found the authorities, in spite of the recent agreement, doing their utmost to prevent the people from entering into trade relations with the English, and scattering broadcast a proclamation threatening death to any Icelander who should so offend. As a result of this proclamation, although it was the season when strangers from the country districts crowded into the capital, Reikevig, for the purposes of barter, none of that class were now to be seen. Mr. Phelps paused for a few days to survey the situation, and then, finding that the authorities were stubbornly resolved not to listen to reason, decisive measures were taken to end the deadlock. Count Tramp, the Danish governor, was seized on a Sunday afternoon and taken under an armed escort on board the *Margaret and Anne* with not the slightest attempt at a rescue, or the least evidence of displeasure, on the part of a number of Icelanders who witnessed his arrest and deposition. Jorgenson, who had played a leading part in this bloodless revolution, promptly entered into possession of Government House, installed himself as head of the state, and commenced his rocket-like career as a miniature Napoleon of the North.*

Jorgenson's first proclamation was dated June 26, 1809, and its opening clause decreed the total abolition of Danish authority in Iceland from that day forth. All Danish officers and persons connected with Danish mercantile houses were strictly enjoined to remain within doors and hold no verbal or written communication with each other. Fire-arms, cutlasses, daggers, ammunition, and the keys of all public and private storehouses were ordered

---

* Sigfrid Schulesen, a native Icelander, published in 1832 a brief history of the revolution, in which he alleged that the reason why Jorgenson's usurpation was not resisted and promptly overthrown was that the guns of the usurper's vessel commanded the capital, Reikevig, which, being built of wood, could readily be set on fire and destroyed. In that case, the general destitution and the absence of shelter in such a severe and inhospitable climate would, he says, have been terrible to contemplate.

to be delivered up at once. "Should these orders
be speedily executed," said the dictator, "it will
save a great deal of unnecessary trouble and the
effusion of blood. But on the contrary, should any
person act in opposition to what is here directed, he
shall immediately be arrested, brought before a
military tribunal, and shot within two hours after
the offence is committed." Finally the native
Icelanders were assured that they had nothing to
fear from the revolution, that they would be treated
in the best possible manner, that nothing but the
true welfare of their country was in view, and that
"our proceedings are solely calculated to insure a
peace and happiness little known to the inhabitants
in later years."

This was speedily followed by a second proclamation declaring Iceland free and independent, and
constituting a representative body to legislate for
the country. All public officers of Icelandic birth
were promised a continuance of their salaries in full
on taking the oath of fidelity in the execution of
their respective functions. Under the new order
of things Iceland would be at peace with all
nations, and Great Britain would become its protector.

Proclamation the third was couched in these truly regal terms :—

" Reikevig, June 29, 1809.

" We are informed that certain evil-minded people have propagated false reports in the country, and have represented to the inhabitants that it is dangerous to travel from place to place, and that much blood has been spilled in the streets of Reikevig by the English. The inhabitants need not be under any apprehension, but may rest assured that no violence will be committed against them, and that they are at full liberty to follow their lawful occupations, without molestation ; and it is hereby declared that all such rumours are entirely without foundation. All persons that do or shall hereafter spread such false reports shall be deemed enemies to the State, and it will be necessary to treat all such people, who do not demean themselves as peaceable citizens, with the utmost severity.

" JORGEN JORGENSON."

A fourth proclamation, under date July 1, 1809, was called forth by a prevalent belief that Jorgenson had decreed a total exemption from the payment of

debts. " It is hereby declared," he explains, " that
only such debt is remitted which is due to the King
of Denmark or to such Danish mercantile houses
whose principals are not residents of Iceland."

The fifth proclamation was the final and decisive
one. It set the seal on the revolution, and was a
sort of Napoleonic *coûp-d'état* in miniature.   It
commenced in these terms :—

"Reikevig, July 11, 1809.

" In our proclamation, dated the 26th of June,
1809, it was requested that the nearest districts
should within a fortnight, and the more distant
within a certain limited time, send in representatives
to consult as to what was best to be done in the
present exigency.   We find, however, that the
public officers have far from facilitated such a
meeting; and we are therefore under the necessity
of no longer resisting the wish of the people, who
have earnestly solicited us to manage the administration of public affairs, and who have in
hundreds offered to serve in the defence of their
country.   It is therefore declared,

" That we, Jorgen Jorgenson, have undertaken

the management of public affairs, under the name
of PROTECTOR, with full power to make war or
conclude peace with foreign powers.

" That the military have nominated us their commander by land and sea, and to regulate the whole
military department in the country.

" That the great seal of the island shall no longer
be respected, but that all public documents of consequence shall be signed by my own hand, and my
seal (J.J.) fixed thereunto.

" That the Icelandic flag shall be blue, with three
white stock-fish thereon, and the honour of it we
promise to defend at the risk of our life and
blood.

" That we have seen with the greatest satisfaction
that the Icelandic clergy, as good Christians, have
promoted tranquillity and good order at this
dangerous period ; therefore, we promise to pay all
their salaries and pensions to clergymen's widows,
and also to improve their present situation as much
as possible.

" That we declare and promise to lay down our
office the moment that the representatives shall be
assembled.   The time appointed for the convocation
of the assembly is the 1st of July, 1810, and we

will then resign, when a proper and suitable consti-
tution shall be agreed upon, and it is declared that
the poor and the common people shall have an
equal share in the government with the rich and
the powerful.

"The situation we now are in requires that
we should not suffer the least disrespect to our
person, neither that anyone should transgress
the least article of this our proclamation, which
has solely in view the welfare of the inhabitants
of this island. We therefore solemnly declare
that the first who shall attempt to disturb the
prosperity or common tranquillity of the country
shall instantly suffer death without benefit of the
civil law.

"All sentences and acts of condemnation must be
signed by us before they can be executed.

                              "JORGEN JORGENSON."

Count Tramp, the deposed Danish Governor, in
his official statement drawn up for the information
of the British Government, declared that "a new
order of things, presenting to view all the miseries
that can spring from boundless despotism, was
forced upon an innocent people, loyal and faithful to

their king." But the events that followed Jorgenson's assumption of supreme authority in Iceland do not corroborate this serious allegation of his predecessor in power. On the contrary, they tend to show that the revolution was popular on the whole, and that the native Icelanders were un- feignedly rejoiced to be relieved from the tyrannies and exactions of the Danish merchants, whose opposition to English traders visiting the island was dictated by a selfish desire to keep up outrageous prices and maintain the monopoly they had so long enjoyed.* Sir William Hooker and the other English eye-witnesses agree in testifying that public business proceeded as usual after Jorgenson had made himself king, that the various governmental officers were paid their salaries punctually, that there were no resignations of any importance by way of protest against the new order of things, that many of the Icelanders offered their services as soldiers to uphold Jorgenson's authority, and that

* Jorgenson exercised undisputed sway over an island of 50,000 inhabitants, whose ancestors had been remarkable for their turbulent and warlike character. The ease with which the revolution was effected and maintained was probably owing in the main to a feeling of satisfaction on the part of the Icelanders at the change. The oppressive laws of the Danes with regard to commerce pressed heavily on the poor. —*Knight.*

the bishop and clergy in synod expressed their satisfaction with the altered situation, declared their willingness to support the new reigning authority, and signed a pastoral letter exhorting all their people to imitate their example.

Having established his authority in the capital, Reikevig, Jorgenson made a modestly regal progress through the country districts, where he apparently was honoured with every mark of popular favour. In the manuscript account of this provincial tour, preserved in the British Museum, Jorgenson says :—

"I travelled by land from the south to the north and the east, accompanied by only five natives, for I needed none to guard me. Everywhere I was received with the greatest cordiality, and I soundly rested in the hospitable hut without fear or danger. The natives regarded me as a real friend and well-wisher of their country. I found many of them suffering under grievous impositions and oppressions, and I speedily redressed all their grievances, established freedom everywhere, and abolished the tyrannous practices that had previously prevailed. After visiting all the northern and eastern ports, I

returned to the south with my little escort, and if
my rule had not been popular, I might have been
easily seized when asleep, but as a matter of fact I
was everywhere welcomed with cheerful countenances by the assembled natives. At one important
town in the north, where a number of Danish
military officers and factors resided, not the
slightest demonstration of hostility was made
against me, for they were afraid of the inhabitants,
who all flocked around me, gave me a cordial
greeting, and earnestly besought me to remedy the
various grievances under which they had long been
groaning."

On returning to Reikevig, fortified by the evident
popularity of his rule in the provinces, and thinking
himself firmly seated in the saddle, Jorgenson
proceeded to vigorously execute his decree for the
confiscation of all Danish property on the island.
The measures he sanctioned in furtherance of this
object were, beyond all doubt, exceedingly harsh and
ruinous to individuals, but like all other usurpers
Jorgenson felt the urgent necessity of reducing to
impotence the enemy within the gates. Not only
was all the property contained in the Danish shops
and warehouses seized and removed, but all the

2

Danish vessels in the harbours, with their cargoes, were captured and manned by Jorgenson's guards. This work of destroying Danish influence in the island, and confiscating Danish property in every shape and form, was still in progress when the revolution was summarily arrested by the unexpected arrival of the British sloop of war, *Talbot*, commanded by the Hon. Alexander Jones. Count Tramp, the deposed governor, who had been kept in close confinement on board the *Margaret and Anne* for a period of nine weeks, succeeded in acquainting the British commander with the treatment to which he had been subjected, and gave him an alarming account of Jorgenson's doings; the despoiled Danish merchants also poured their grievances into the sympathetic ear of Captain Jones, and besought him to check the wild and wilful career of the audacious usurper. Acting on these representations, the commander of the *Talbot* officially communicated with Mr. Phelps, whom he regarded as the primary and chief instigator of recent revolutionary events, the Warwick, the King-maker of Iceland. Mr. Phelps replied with a brief statement of the reasons (summarised in a previous page) that impelled him to the deposition of the Danish governor. This statement was deemed far from satisfactory by Captain Jones, and, as it seemed to him that the honour of England was involved in the matter, he issued a peremptory letter to Mr. Phelps that had the effect of overturning the throne of King Jorgenson and closing a remarkable chapter in the modern history of Iceland. In this decisive communication the British commander severely observed:

"I also conceive it my duty to acquaint you that, from your not having any other authority that I am aware of, besides being owner of a letter of marque, you appear to me to have far exceeded that authority by taking on you the government of an island not actually considered hostile to Great Britain, the wretched state of whose inhabitants His Majesty has been graciously pleased so far to relieve in winter as to grant licenses to you, and even to the enemies of Great Britain, to support them. You have, in my opinion, not only transgressed the laws of Great Britain, but of all nations, by assuming an authority which no subject of any realm whatever can have a right to—namely, that of declaring the island free, neutral, independent,

2*

and at peace with all nations, and of appointing a
Governor who is not a British subject, but a Dane,
who has been an apprentice on board an English
collier, who served his time as a midshipman in His
Majesty's navy, who afterwards fought against Great
Britain, and was made a prisoner by an English ship
of war. I understand he has issued, with your
sanction, proclamations signed in a regal manner,
(' We, Jorgen Jorgenson,'); besides which he has,
in sight of His Majesty's ship under my command,
hoisted a flag as yet unknown, and he is at this
moment employed in erecting a battery within
musket-shot without my permission, and even
without having consulted me on the subject, which
is not only taking up arms against his own country
(Denmark) but a disrespect to my pendant. I feel
myself called upon therefore to notice his conduct,
which no attachment or zeal Mr. Jorgenson may
have for Great Britain can countenance, neither
would it, I am sure, meet with the approbation of
the British Government. I now most earnestly
recommend, either that you do not leave the whole
power in the island in the hands of Mr. Jorgenson
alone (however qualified or respectable his character
may be) until His Majesty's pleasure is known, or

that you immediately restore the former mode of
government, giving the supreme command to some
of the most respectable of the inhabitants of the
island. Having thus, according to my duty, acquainted you with my sentiments, and pointed out
the line of conduct that I conceive you, as a British
subject, ought to adopt, I shall not interfere farther
than by requesting to be acquainted with your
future intentions, for the information of the Right
Honourable the Lords Commissioners of the
Admiralty. You are wrong in supposing that I
wish to cast any stain upon your character, either as
an Englishman or a man of honour, nor can I
believe you would intentionally commit an act
which would reflect disgrace upon the British
Government. I am also far from doubting the
word of Mr. Jorgenson, or from throwing any
reflections either on his former situation, his
character or conduct; but his not possessing any
written document to certify that he has permission
from the British Government to be on this island,
and his having appeared on board His Majesty's
ship under my command in the undress uniform of
a post-captain, oblige me to insist on his immediate
return to Great Britain, unless you can satisfy

me that you have permission to bring him
here. "

Mr. Phelps was unable to give the requisite
satisfaction to the British Commander, and, as
Jorgenson was not prepared to fight against
England in defence of his throne, he had no other
alternative than to abdicate. An agreement was
entered into by all the parties concerned, by which
the Government of Iceland was temporarily entrusted to the hands of its two most influential
residents (the Chief Justice and the Sheriff of the
Western county), who accepted the responsibility of
guarding the persons and property of all British
subjects on the island. The ex-king and the
deposed Danish Governor then sailed for London in
different ships, the former to justify his action in
gratuitously enrolling himself amongst the reigning
monarchs, and the latter to ventilate his grievances
before the British Government. On the third day
of the voyage, the vessel that carried the Governor
was found to be on fire, and Jorgenson providentially
bore up just in time to save all on board from a
frightful fate. " We were but too happy," says Sir
William Hooker, who was one of the passengers on

the doomed vessel, "to escape with our lives and with the clothes upon our backs, and even for this we were in no small degree indebted to the extraordinary exertions of Mr. Jorgenson at a time when nearly the whole of the ship's crew seemed paralysed with fear. He, too, as would be expected by all who knew his character, was the last to quit the burning vessel."

When they eventually arrived in London, Jorgenson established himself at his old quarters—the Spread Eagle Inn, Gracechurch Street, and reported himself to the Lords of the Admiralty. Count Tramp, the Danish Governor, lost no time in sending to the same tribunal a furious indictment of the ex-king and a detailed account of all the indignities to which he had been subjected by the orders of the usurper. The original manuscript of the latter is now preserved in the British Museum.

The Count had decidedly the best of the argument in the end, for, although he did not succeed in getting all the satisfaction he desired, he was sufficiently placated to gratefully acknowledge that "the peculiar favour which Iceland and its concerns have met with here, and the manner in which His British Majesty's Ministers have interested them-

selves in its welfare, and above all the security
obtained for the future, has entirely obliterated all
bitterness from my heart." Poor Jorgenson, on the
other hand, was soon arrested, not for the superior
and stately crime of having unlawfully made himself
king of Iceland, but for the vulgar and commonplace offence of having left England without permission whilst he was a prisoner on parole. He was
at first confined in Tothill Fields prison and subsequently transferred to the hulks that were moored
off Chatham, in which a considerable number of
foreign prisoners of war were under temporary
detention. Here he had to endure many miseries,
privations and disappointments, before he was
restored to partial freedom. In the meantime the
British Government had issued a proclamation,
practically making Iceland neutral territory during
the continuance of the war, specifically exempting
it from attack, and pledging protection to all ships
engaged in direct trade between Iceland and
British ports. Sir William Hooker not unreasonably
claims that Jorgenson's *coup d'état* was thus "the
means of placing the island in a greater state of
security than formerly," and that it "had opened a
way for bettering the condition of its inhabitants."

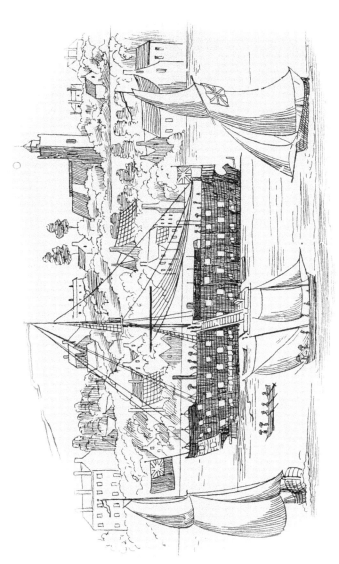

"A FLOATING PRISON."

(From the original drawing by J. JORGENSON, in the Egerton Collection at the British Museum.)

Success or the absence of it is the one standard by which revolutions are judged. Jorgenson's was successful as far as it went, and also in the indirect benefits to the Icelanders that it was chiefly instrumental in bringing about. But, as it was nipped in the bud before Jorgenson could mature his plans or give general effect to his policy, it is impossible to say what sort of a reputation he would have achieved as a ruler had he been permitted to govern the country for a longer period. In his defence in London before the Lords of the Admiralty he stoutly maintained that he had established liberty in Iceland without shedding a drop of blood or committing a single man to prison ; further, that he had bestowed all the blessings of free-trade upon the country and opened up the brightest prospects to a long oppressed people. Sir William Hooker, too, states that " among the improvements which it was Mr. Jorgenson's intention to have made in the island, had he been permitted to retain his office, that of bettering the miserable condition of the scholars was not the least meritorious or of the least importance."

For his brief-butterfly escapade as an unlicensed monarch in Iceland, Jorgenson suffered a severe

penalty in the shape of twelve months' close
confinement, and, what was far worse than the mere
deprivation of liberty, he contracted vicious habits
in prison that prejudicially affected the whole of
his after-life. He became a confirmed gambler and,
after his release, lost every penny he possessed by
foolishly frequenting the haunts of the London card-
sharpers. He scraped up from the wreck of his
affairs sufficient to carry him to Lisbon, and for a
time led a romantic existence in Spain and Portugal,
being once arrested as a suspicious character by
order of General Trant. On returning to Lisbon, he
found himself unable to resist the fascination of the
gaming-tables and was once again reduced to
destitution. By shipping as a common seaman on
board a British gun-boat, Jorgenson temporarily
placed himself beyond the reach of temptation, and,
after having participated in several engagements,
he was invalided home. We next get a glimpse of
him as the guest of his friend, Sir William Hooker,
at Halesworth, in Suffolk, where, amidst rural
delights and far removed from the fatal pitfalls of
city life, he dwelt for a season in what must have
been an atmosphere of strange serenity and calm to
such a stormy petrel as he. It was in this secluded

spot he wrote his history of the Icelandic revolution. On returning to London he unfortunately fell in with his old evil associates, spent his nights in the gambling dens, was once more plucked of every feather, and found himself eventually in the Fleet prison under arrest for debt.

Jorgenson was still a prisoner at the Fleet when the second singular episode of his life occurred, and a splendid opportunity was afforded him of retrieving his falling fortunes. A Government messenger sought him out one day, and told him he was wanted at the Foreign Office. He hastened to Downing Street, had an interview with a personage high in authority, and accepted service on a secret mission to the Continent. A certain amount of mystery surrounds this suddenly-conceived and rapidly-executed embassy. Jorgenson himself describes its object somewhat vaguely, as an effort " to ascertain what effects the subjugation of the troops of Napoleon was likely to have in advancing the interests of British commerce," but it is certain that he did not confine his inquiries and observations to this ostensible purpose. With his debt discharged and his purse replenished by the Foreign Office, Jorgenson's prospects were now comparatively

bright; but, once more, his unfortunate gambling
propensities were very nearly proving his ruin.
He lost all his ready money, but succeeded by a
subterfuge in crossing over from Gravesend to
Ostend in the garb of a sailor.   Landed on the
Continent, he was at liberty to draw on the Foreign
Office for his travelling expenses, and having thus
re-filled his empty pocket, he pushed on and arrived
in time to witness the battle of Waterloo.   Proceeding to Paris, he was engaged in diplomatic
work there for some time, and apparently acquitted
himself satisfactorily, for the Foreign Office entered
into a second agreement with him to travel through
France and Germany to Warsaw, and make an
inquiry into Polish affairs.   Just as in London, he
could not leave Paris without a farewell visit to his
favourite gambling resorts.   He had no intention
of playing, but the fatal fascination of the scene
proved irresistible.   He was a winner at first, but
the chapter of his Parisian gambling experiences
closed by leaving him literally destitute, and a
bleak December morn beheld the ex-king quitting
the French metropolis on foot, in a very woe-begone
condition.   For nearly the whole of the period
during which he was touring through France and

Germany, Jorgenson lived by his wits, and the record of his shifts and subterfuges, his audacities and perplexities, is one of the most amusing in the annals of itinerant vagabondage. It will be found in full in subsequent pages. In the course of his peregrinations, Jorgenson made the acquaintance of the illustrious Goethe, also Marshal Blucher, Niebuhr, Bernstorf, and the Prince Von Muskaw.

On returning to London, Jorgenson was favourably received at the Foreign Office, and handsomely rewarded for his diplomatic labours on the Continent, the authorities apparently being wholly unaware of the happy-go-lucky circumstances under which he had fulfilled his mission. Possibly it was a case of good coming out of evil. The fact that he was rendered penniless by his gambling indiscretions, and thereby compelled to travel after the fashion of the pilgrims of old doubtless brought him into contact with a number of useful people, and enabled him to extract a variety of valuable information that might not otherwise have been procurable.

With the substantial sum he received from the Foreign Office, in recognition of his Continental services, Jorgenson formed the good resolution of emigrating to America, and settling down to a steady life at last. But once more he fell a victim to his besetting sin, and the consequences this time were disastrous. He abandoned himself to the worship of the fickle goddess who presides over the chances of the cards, and for a considerable period lived the feverish life, and experienced all the vicissitudes of the London gambler in those high-pressure days. Looking back upon this madly-reckless, hot-headed, and sadly-wasted time, from the calm contemplative standpoint of his An-tipodean exile, Jorgenson pronounced it to be the darkest stage of his existence—" a painful period of disheartening dissipation." It ended by bringing him within the pale of the law. He was arrested for illegally disposing of certain articles of furniture appertaining to his lodgings in Tottenham Court Road, was tried at the Old Bailey, convicted, and sentenced to seven years' transportation beyond the seas.

This sentence, however, was not immediately carried into effect. Jorgenson had powerful friends at Court, who retained a grateful remembrance of his services in bygone days, and through their influence, instead of being forthwith banished to

the Antipodes, he was appointed hospital assistant
in Newgate, where he remained for twenty months,
safe from the assaults of his ruinous temptation,
and enjoying, in his own words, " a happy and
contented life." He exhibited his wonted versatility
by supervising the spiritual as well as the bodily
health of the prisoners. Some of the sermons he
preached in Newgate are still to be seen in the
British Museum, and a few extracts from them are
given in subsequent pages. Jorgenson's experiences
in this historic London prison are set forth at some
length in his autobiography, and will be found to
comprise not a few singular incidents and suggestive
observations.

Released at the end of twenty months, on condition that he quitted the country within one month
from the day of his liberation, Jorgenson, the in_
corrigible, repaired to his old haunts with the
celerity of the moth towards the candle, and was at
last consumed in the flame. He overstayed his
allotted time, gambled away his little all, and was
hurrying to the docks to leave England for ever,
when he unluckily met an old acquaintance on
Tower Hill, who invited him to his house and then
basely betrayed him into the hands of the

authorities, with the result that poor Jorgenson, the victim of misplaced confidence, had his doom sealed by a sentence of death, subsequently commuted to transportation for life.

The ex-king of Iceland was one of 150 convicts, under a strong military guard, on board the chartered ship *Woodman*, that sailed from Sheerness to Van Diemen's Land, in November, 1825. But he was a privileged personage here, no less than he was in Newgate. He was appointed to the post of dispenser in the ship's hospital, and was accorded the freedom of the deck from sunrise to sunset.

Before the voyage was far advanced, a sad event was the means of temporarily promoting him to a much higher and more responsible position, for the surgeon of the ship was one day seized by brain fever, and suddenly expired. In this unlooked-for emergency the medical knowledge and experience acquired by Jorgenson in Newgate became invaluable, and he was therefore placed in charge of the ship's hospital for the nonce. Whether the credit was due to good luck, or the skilful treatment of the amateur doctor, it is impossible to say, but it is certain that when the vessel arrived at the Cape she

was in a position to present a clean bill of health,
and to report that there was not a single patient in
the hospital. Jorgenson was complimented on the
success with which he had filled, for five weeks, the
vacant post, and received some informal assurance
that his services as acting-physician would not be
forgotten—a promise that he bitterly complained in
after days bore but little advantageous fruit for
him.

The Admiral at the Cape sent one of his own
surgeons to supply the vacancy on the *Woodman*,
and the voyage to Van Diemen's Land was resumed.
Hobart, the charmingly - situated capital of that
colony, was reached early in May, and Jorgenson
was naturally deeply moved at the first sight of a
city which he had assisted in founding 23 years
before, when he was a young British naval officer.
Now he was an exiled convict, and bitterly did he
bewail his reckless pursuit of a passion that had
brought him to this unhappy fate.

On the morning after the *Woodman* had
anchored, Jorgenson and his fellow-convicts were
paraded before the Governor, Sir George Arthur,
and assigned to various employers, who had need of
their services. Jorgenson himself was appointed to

3

a clerkship in the Government offices at Hobart, but routine work of that description did not suit his restless temperament, and he applied for a transfer to the service of the Van Diemen's Land Company, a wealthy corporation, two of whose London directors had favoured him with letters of recommendation to their principal representative in the colony. The Government refused his application at first, but eventually consented. He was attached to several parties that had been organised for the purpose of exploring and opening up the Company's extensive territory, and his adventures by flood and field, amongst blacks and bushrangers, constitute not the least stirring chapter in the history of this extraordinary character.

On returning to civilisation again, we find him editing a newspaper in the metropolis for a short time, but he soon returned to the more congenial roving life of the country. On the nomination of Sir George Arthur, he proceeded to the district of Oatlands to take up the joint appointment of constable in the field police, and assistant-clerk in the local court. His district was no less than 150 miles in circumference, and its scattered inhabitants were terrorised by hostile blacks and sanguinary white

desperadoes. Many of the latter he ran down and
captured, exhibiting conspicuous pluck and perseverance and a characteristic disregard of danger and
difficulty. The local magistrates were enthusiastic
in their praises of his untiring energy and zeal in the
pursuit of the outlaws. The Hon. Thomas Anstey,
M.P., chief magistrate of the Oatlands district,
publicly testified to his "honesty and fearlessness in
the discharge of arduous duties." The Hon. M.
Forster, M.P., declared that he had "rendered great
services to the community by his successful pursuit
of bushrangers," and several other justices of the
peace bore witness from personal knowledge that he
had been chiefly instrumental in breaking up
notorious gangs of marauders. Still, all the while
he was rendering these valuable services, he was
himself nominally a prisoner, but on opening the
Government Gazette one day he had the satisfaction
of seeing that stigma removed by the official proclamation of his pardon.

Soon afterwards, Sir George Arthur devised his
famous, but futile, scheme for the suppression of
the hostile blacks, whose incessant attacks on the
settlers had become a standing menace to the peace
and prosperity of the colony. He called out the

3*

whole available white population, provided them
with arms and ammunition, and established a
military cordon right across the island. His object
was to hem the blacks in and drive them before him
into a narrow-necked peninsula at the south-western
corner of the colony, where they could be easily
captured and removed to an island in Bass Straits
that was in every way suitable for their main-
tenance. This campaign, known in colonial history
as "The Black War," was a colossal and costly
failure. The cunning and agility of the blacks
defeated the superior numbers and organisation of
the whites. At the same time the campaign undoubtedly infused a certain amount of wholesome
fear into the minds of the natives, and paved
the way for their early pacification through the
agencies of kindness and philanthropy. Jorgenson was entrusted with a command in the "Black
War," and, in reward for his services, received
a grant of 100 acres of land with a promise
from the Colonial Secretary that this area would
be increased by a further free gift if he turned
it to good account. By holding out this inducement the authorities hoped that he would be
led to settle on the soil, but, with his customary

recklessness, no sooner did he obtain possession
of his land than he turned it into ready money,
which speedily took unto itself wings. A legacy
of £500 in money and property, which he received
from relatives in Denmark, slipped through his
fingers after a similar fashion. He added to his
thoughtless imprudences by wedding a termagant
wife; his latter days were passed in privation and
obscurity, and he closed his extraordinary and
eventful career in the Hobart Hospital in the sixty-
fifth year of his age.

Jorgenson is a striking instance of a man of considerable natural abilities making shipwreck of his
life through a lamentable lack of ballast, aggravated
by culpably-erratic steering. He himself, in one of
his letters to Sir William Hooker, candidly confesses :—

"I have foolishly rejected the many excellent
opportunities of advancing my fortune in this world
which I certainly have possessed."

With the celebrity he acquired by virtue of
his daring revolutionary achievement in Iceland,
the patronage subsequently accorded him by the

British Foreign Office, the *prestige* of his successful diplomatic missions on the Continent, and
the acquaintance of the eminent men with whom
he had official intercourse in France and Germany, Jorgenson could have easily ascended the
ladder of honourable distinction, had he but refrained from his ruinous vice of gambling, and
marked out for himself a steady and systematic
course of action. Sir William Hooker, who had
the best and most intimate opportunities of study-
ing his character and gauging his capacities, does
not hesitate to say that Jorgenson " had talents of
the highest order."

Mr. Fenton, the historian of Tasmania, describes
him as a " clever but unscrupulous man "; the Rev.
Sabine Baring-Gould is less complimentary, and
sums him up as " a thorough adventurer ready for
any emergency," whilst Marcus Clarke considers him
" a singularly accomplished fortune-wooer—one of
the most interesting human comets recorded in
history." That he was endowed by nature with a
more than ordinary share of serviceable qualities—
that he was exceptionally energetic, enterprising,
clever, courageous, astute, affable, intelligent, keen-
witted and wonderfully versatile—the record of his

variegated career abundantly shows; but it is no less certain that all his natural advantages profited him nothing, that he was a rudderless barque from the beginning to the end of his voyage, and that, notwithstanding brave show and full sail and sun-lit seas from time to time, he eventually and inevitably came to disastrous and irretrievable ruin on the rocks. So the moral of his life-story is a simple and familiar one. Talents and opportunities are bestowed in vain when a man subjects himself to the slavery of a despotic passion. In his faraway Antipodean exile, casting a retrospective glance at his chequered career in the northern hemisphere, and recalling how different his fate might have been if he had exercised greater stability and self-control, poor Jorgenson might well be forgiven if he had thundered, in the graphic lines of Talfourd, against gambling as a vice

—" which no affections urge,
And no delights refine; which from the soul
Steals mounting impulses which might inspire
Its noblest virtues, for the arid quest
Of wealth 'mid ruin; changes enterprise
To squalid greediness, makes heaven-born hope
A shivering fever, and in vile collapse
Leaves the exhausted heart without one fibre
Impell d by generous passion."

CHAPTER I.

WHO so able to write a man's life as the living man
himself? The age of intellect has merged into the
autobiographical. A Homer is no longer wanting to
immortalise an Agamemnon. For where is now
the man not qualified to sing his own praise, to
sound the trumpet of his own exploits—or who like
myself would suffer the sad but instructive vicissitudes of his fate to pass by unwept and unrecorded,
or, as Horace says, wrapped up in the darkness of a
long and silent night—*illacrymabiles?* No! Having
been promised a niche in *Ross's Van Diemen's Land
Annual*, the only sanctuary and safe retreat of
great names, the sole Westminster Abbey which these
Australian regions can yet boast, I hasten to fill it
up, before a greater man steps in to occupy the
ground.

It is curious that the most important event of a man's life should ever rest upon secondary evidence. No one, however, will dispute the fact that I was born in the city of Copenhagen in the year 1780. My father, who was a mathematical instrument maker in good repute,* sent me early to school, and, though I say it myself, I was no bad scholar. We have very good schools in Denmark, and the industry of the boys is stimulated by periodical rewards, which are distributed by the ministers of state. On one occasion—I shall never forget it—one of my school-fellows, a tall, overbearing boy whom I had repeatedly conquered in the class, took occasion to insult me, though he was really twice my size, very grossly in the street. I immediately offered him battle, but the cowardly fellow, seeing the gate of the Round Tower open, near which the occurrence took place, ran in, probably thinking that I would not venture to follow him. This tower was originally built by Christian IV. as an

* Jorgenson came from a family of learned watchmakers long established in Copenhagen. His father, also named Jorgen Jorgenson, held the appointment of watch and clock maker to the Court of Denmark; his elder brother, Urban, published an exhaustive quarto volume on the measurement of time; and his nephew, Louis Urban, is the author of a series of standard works on the art of watch-making.

observatory, and though of great height is ascended by a spiral road sufficiently sloping as to admit the ascent of carriages. Up this my adversary ran, and I after him at full speed. When near the top, whom should we meet but the king, accompanied by one of his ministers, descending in a carriage. In the heat of pursuit, I brushed past, as I hoped without being observed, and reached the summit. There I engaged my opponent, but being out of breath after my run up the eminence, was cruelly beaten. As luck would have it, this incident happened on the day before the public examination and distribution of prizes, and though I acquitted myself to the satisfaction of my teachers, I lost my reward from the hands of the minister, who had witnessed my disorderly conduct in the Round Tower on the previous day.

I had attained the age of fourteen when the dreadful conflagration of the king's enormous palace of Christianburgh took place. The flames that issued from the immense pile, awful as they were, filled my youthful mind with the most lively emotions of delight. I never contemplated for a moment the destruction of property in the striking magnificence of the scene. At night the spectacle

was truly grand, and I stood looking on with unwearied pleasure as the devouring element continued
its ravages. One after another the roofs of the
beautiful halls fell in, scarcely leaving time to
remove any of the valuable furniture. As I stood
on a little eminence, I watched in particular the
destruction of the great Hall of Knights, filled with
full-length portraits of ancient Danish heroes, and
as the crackling canvasses swelled out and yielded to
the flames, it seemed as if the figures became
animated and were moving from their long
imprisonment against the walls. The numerous
lakes and ornamental waters, with which this fine
city is surrounded, reflected the soaring and leap-
ing flames, and contributed greatly to the majesty
of the scene. The fire raged furiously for three
successive days and nights, and the once mighty
edifice smoked and smouldered in its own ruins for
more than a month. The palace was situated upon
an island to which access could only be had by
means of drawbridges. A singular feature in the
scene was the assistance rendered by the Dutchmen
of Amager in the unavailing efforts to extinguish
the fire. In that little island a small colony
from Holland had been permitted to settle by

Frederick II. The island is close to Copenhagen, and although more than 300 years have elapsed, its inhabitants continue to wear the dress, to speak the language, and in every respect to practise the original habits of their Dutch ancestors, feeding dairy cows and supplying Copenhagen with milk and vegetables. The very sight of a Dutchman in his woollen jacket and single - leg canvas petticoats suggests the idea of wading in water, and at the fire this little Dutch colony turned out *en masse* with buckets to contribute their humble but futile efforts towards arresting the progress of the flames. The king himself, Christian II. an eccentric man, was hardly able to realize the terrible truth that his everlasting palace, as he thought, was being reduced to ashes, and force had to be employed to remove him from his burning chamber.

As a boy in Copenhagen I saw so many ships from foreign climes that my mind had become insensibly imbued with an ardent desire to go to sea and visit other countries. When I beheld a Danish Indiaman set sail with its officers on deck, dressed in their attractive uniforms, my heart burned with envy, and it appeared to my susceptible imagination that there

could be no enjoyment greater than that of gliding
over the smooth waters in an immense ship, among
new men and new scenes, presenting pictures of
endless novelty and delight. My father, perhaps to
sicken me of these nautical yearnings, had me bound
apprentice on an English collier, which had brought
a cargo from Newcastle for the use of the Copenhagen
blacksmiths. On this vessel I served for four years,
trading to the Baltic in summer and to London in
the winter, and although during that period I tasted
little of the cream of life, yet I became thoroughly
acquainted with sea affairs, mastered the art of
navigation, became proficient in the English
language, read a great many books and saw something
of London when I had leave to go ashore.

Having attained the age of eighteen and commenced to think for myself (for we in Denmark are
of age at sixteen), I quitted the collier and engaged
with a South Sea whaler which was going out with
stores to the Cape of Good Hope. There I made a
fresh engagement with Captain Black of the schooner
Harbinger, bound for Algoa Bay, also with
government stores. Captain Black was an intelligent
enterprising man, the son of a clergyman in Suffolk.
He had been the purser of the *Jane Shore* when

that convict transport was piratically seized by the prisoners and soldiers on the voyage to Botany Bay. They mutinied in mid ocean, murdered the captain and most of the crew, and steered the vessel to Buenos Ayres. Black managed to escape from his cot in the dark, while the ruffians were dealing slaughter around, and thus fortunately he escaped the carnage. One of the prisoners, "Major" Sempill, of light-fingered celebrity, offered a desperate resistance to the mutineers, and had his courageous and praiseworthy conduct been promptly seconded by the military, this daring act of piracy would not in all probability have been successfully consummated. Sempill and eighteen others, who refused to cast in their lot with the mutineers, were put into a boat, and, after many hardships and deprivations at sea under a burning sun, succeeded in reaching the West Indies. Black found his way back to England and then proceeded to the Cape, where he obtained the command of the *Harbinger*, which was now starting with stores for the forces stationed at Algoa Bay to defend the settlers from the attacks of the Kaffirs. On arriving there we found H.M.S. *Rattlesnake*, 22 guns, and the *Camel*, a reduced 44, lying at anchor in the bay.

In the evening, after everything had been adjusted on deck, I was ordered to take a boat and visit the English man-of-war. As I approached the side of what I thought was the British vessel and was about to ascend, I heard people on deck conversing in a language then strange to my ears. I speedily drew back and returned to the *Harbinger*. It was not long before we discovered that it was the French ship *La Preneuse* of 44 guns, which had watched the two British vessels coming into the bay, and not suspecting them to be armed, had entered unobserved in the dusk of the evening and anchored alongside, expecting to make easy prizes both of them and our schooner. The captains of the *Rattlesnake* and the *Camel*, not anticipating any occurrence of this kind, had both gone on shore for the night, and had no means of regaining their ships, which they eagerly wished to do as soon as they heard the guns in the engagement that speedily commenced. The fight lasted for six hours during the night, until the Frenchman taking advantage of a land breeze, ran out to the open sea.

On my return to the Cape I joined the brig *Lady Nelson*, Lieutenant Grant, a small surveying vessel of sixty-five tons appointed as a tender to Captain

Flinders, of the *Investigator*. The *Lady Nelson*, though small, was very comfortably fitted up, and having been built expressly for the voyage, was admirably adapted for the purpose intended. She drew only four feet of water and was fitted with a remarkable sliding keel, the invention of Commissioner Shanks, of the Navy Board, which answered so well that I have often wondered it has not come into more general use. It was composed of three posts or broad planks, fitted into three corresponding sockets or openings which went completely through the vessel from the deck to the keel. These planks could be let down or drawn up at pleasure to a depth of eight feet, according as the vessel went into deep or shallow water, or, when sailing against the wind, to obviate the leeway. We were under orders to proceed to the south of Australia and ascertain definitely whether the straits now called Bass's, separating Australia from Van Diemen's Land, really existed. Dr. Bass had adventurously voyaged from Sydney to Western Port in a whaleboat, but it was still undetermined whether Van Diemen's Land was really an island, wholly separated by water from Australia.

From observations made by Dr. Bass during his

excursion, he gave it as his decided opinion that
some strait must exist in that quarter. To clear
up the doubtful point, Captain Flinders, accompanied by Dr. Bass, set sail from Sydney, but
before the result of their expedition was known in
England, the *Lady Nelson* was despatched with the
same object, Lieutenant Grant being instructed to
shape his course for the same latitude, in order to
enter at the western extremity of this strait, should
it prove to be really existent. The first point we
made was King's Island, which had escaped the
notice of Captain Flinders. We sailed round it,
and named it after the then governor of New South
Wales, Captain King, R.N. Our discovery of this
passage lessened the distance to Sydney from the
Cape and other places to the westward by some
hundreds of miles, and superseded the necessity in
the stormy seasons of running down a high
southern latitude. From King's Island we proceeded to Sydney, afterwards returning to complete
the survey of Port Phillip, Western Port, Port
Dalrymple, and the Derwent. We next accompanied Captain Flinders and the *Investigator* on an
expedition to the northern shores of Australia.
On reaching the Northumberland Islands, situated

4

about 1,500 miles north of Sydney, we had the
misfortune to lose all our anchors and cables on the
coral reefs, and were obliged to steer for the main
island of the chain, where we found a good harbour.
Necessity is truly said to be the mother of invention,
for here we made, what in other circumstances we
should never have thought of, an anchor out of the
heaviest wood we could find on shore. It was one
third of the whole length of the vessel, and we
loaded it with about 200 lbs. of lead on the crown.
Though it proved the salvation of the vessel, it was
exceedingly awkward from its great size, and very
difficult to draw up. The *Investigator* was in
consequence obliged to proceed on her surveying
expedition without us. She had several naturalists
and scientific gentlemen on board, amongst them
the indefatigable Mr. R. Brown, the talented
botanist and author of the best work yet extant on
the plants of these colonies, the *Prodromus Novæ
Hollandiæ* ; Mr. Bauer, the eminent German painter
and draughtsman employed by Sir Joseph Banks ;
Mr. Cartall, the English landscape painter, and
Mr. Kelly, a distinguished botanist, sent out at the
expense of Sir Joseph Banks. On our return to
Sydney, we were compelled to allow the *Lady*

Nelson to run on shore, for our wooden anchor had become so dry, from lying on the gunwales in that latitude for five weeks of very warm weather, that, when we attempted to cast it, on our approach to Sydney, it could not be made to sink.

When the *Investigator* had completed the circumnavigation of Australia, she was condemned at Sydney, as unfit for further service, though I thought at the time she was a very good ship. If she had been my property, I would certainly not have condemned her. But there are reasons for everything, except for getting drunk, which the greatest drunkards themselves admit to be the most unreasonable act that a reasonable man can commit, and the *Investigator* was accordingly cut down and sent home to England, under the care of Captain Kent, R.N. This gentleman was originally captain of the *Buffalo,* and a lieutenant under Admiral Byng, who was shot for not bringing the enemy to battle at Minorca, while the Admiral of the French fleet ran away and was handsomely rewarded for his pains. Captain Kent was the only lieutenant under Admiral Byng who was afterwards promoted. He married the niece of Captain Hunter, R.N., the second governor of New South

4*

Wales. Hunter was the captain of the ship which brought out Captain Phillip, the first Australian governor. Captain King, the third governor, was second lieutenant of the same ship. At first King was sent to Norfolk Island as commandant. When he became Governor, he acquired a celebrity for eccentricities. One day at Parramatta he was waited on by two prisoners suing for pardons. One presented a petition signed by all the leading men of Sydney, whilst the petition of the other bore the signature of one only.

"How comes it," said the Governor, "that you have only one name to your petition, whilst this man has so many?"

"I have lived," the man replied, "with only one master all my time, sir, and I did not know anybody else."

The Governor immediately gave this man a pardon, but the other applicant was dismissed, with the remark that "as you already know so many rich friends, you don't need one."

On another occasion a country settler waited on Governor King, to request the loan of a prisoner to assist him in shingling his house.

"Come to me," said the Governor, "in six

weeks' time, when the harvest is over, and I will find a man for you."

At the end of the stipulated period, the settler, who did not enjoy a reputation for indefatigable personal industry, again presented himself.

" Go into that room," said the Governor, " and you will see your man."

After a few moments, the settler returned, saying that he could not find the man, although he had looked all over the room, even under the table and behind the sofa.

"Not find him!" cried the Governor, " how is that? Come along with me, and I'll soon find him for you."

Then leading the settler a second time into the room, the Governor made him look into a large mirror over the mantelpiece, saying, " That is the man to shingle your house; take him with you, quick! and see that he does it."

CHAPTER II.

AT that early period in the history of New South
Wales, owing to the infrequency of supplies from
England, provisions and other articles of consump-
tion were often sold at enormous prices. It was
no uncommon thing to give ten guineas for a
gallon of rum, tolerably diluted. Tobacco was
proportionately dear, and tea was never under a
guinea a pound. Money itself sympathised with
the general rise. The common penny pieces
passed for two-pence, and half-pence for pence. A
large quantity of copper was speculatively brought
out from England by shipmasters, who thus realised
a profit of 100 per cent. without the smallest
trouble; the colony ultimately became most incon-
veniently loaded with copper money. The evil was

worse than in the days of Wood's half-pence, which
Dean Swift so ably suppressed, and Governor King
was eventually compelled to put his veto on the
further introduction of such money. He speedily
settled the difficulty by reducing pence and half-
pence to their real value.

It was in 1803 that we set sail from Sydney with
Captain Bowen, R.N., as commandant, to assist in
establishing a settlement on the Derwent, in
Van Diemen's Land. The late Dr. Mountgarrett
and two ladies, whose names I have still the
pleasure of enrolling in the number of my friends,
accompanied us on the expedition. We disem-
barked our passengers and stores on the north
bank of the Derwent at Risdon. Proceeding to
Port Phillip on the southern coast of Australia,
where Colonel Collins had vainly attempted to
form a settlement, owing to the aridity of the soil
and the distressing scarcity of fresh water, we took
the Colonel and his officials on board our little
vessel. The ship *Ocean* sailed in company with us,
having on board the colonel's men stores, and
from 300 to 400 prisoners. She sailed so badly
that we were obliged to assist her in coming up the
Derwent.

During our absence, the temporary establishment at Risdon was found to be ineligible, and the present site of Hobart Town was ultimately selected for the permanent settlement. We landed at Sullivan's Cove and pitched our tents. Spades, hoes, saws and axes were put into the hands of the prisoners, and we commenced clearing away as fast as we could. As I walk up and down the streets of this now large and populous town, the recollection of the primeval wildness of the scene as I first saw it 32 years ago fills me with conflicting emotions. The spot on which the Bank of Van Diemen's Land and the Hope and Anchor now stand, was then an inpervious grove of the thickest brushwood, surmounted with some of the largest gum-trees that this island could produce. All along the rivulet as far as the present site of the Upper Mill, was impassable from the denseness of the shrubbery and underwood, the huge collections of prostrate trees, and the dead timber which had been washed down by the stream and strewn all around. These had in parts blocked up the channel, and many places that are now dry and built upon, or cultivated in fruitful gardens, were then covered with rushes and water.

The *Lady Nelson* was now commanded by Lieutenant Simmons, under whom I had the honour of serving as chief officer. Having completed our duties at the Derwent, we were despatched to Port Dalrymple to survey the entrance of the Tamar. As a result of our report, Colonel Paterson was sent from headquarters in a small cutter with prisoners and stores, to form a settlement at Georgetown. We next proceeded to King's Island, the survey of which we accomplished. We found the large species of seal, known as the sea elephant, crowding every part of the shore, and some beautiful specimens of the emu enlivened the open parts of the interior. The race of these interesting birds, I am sorry to say, has become extinct in King's Island, owing to the constant and harassing attacks of the sealers. After visiting and surveying Kent's Group and laying down the soundings along the channel of Bass's Strait, we returned to Sydney, where we re-equipped and sailed with the establishment for the new settlement at Newcastle, situated about 70 miles to the north of Sydney, a place rich in coals, cedar and fish.

After finishing our work at Newcastle, I left His

Majesty's service and took charge of a sealer on a
trip to New Zealand. We killed several thousands
of these harmless creatures. It is indeed astonish-
ing to notice with what eagerness the sailors enter
into this pursuit, knocking down the seals with
their clubs, stripping them of their skins, and
pegging them out to dry or salting them down in
casks with the utmost zeal and perseverance. At
that time sealskins sold in London at a guinea
each. We filled our little vessel and returned to
Sydney. My next experience was as chief officer
of a whaler, the *Alexander*. We sailed for the
Derwent, and I can boast of having struck the first
whale in that river. Had its brothers and sisters
been warned by the violent death to which their near
relation was thus subjected, and avoided the fatal
spot for the future, I would have little hope of
living in the grateful remembrance of future
whalers; but the contrary is the case, for the
destruction of one apparently attracted many
hundreds of others to crowd up and incur the same
fate, and the rising city of Hobart Town is yearly
and rapidly becoming enriched on their oleaginous
remains.

From the Derwent we proceeded to Norfolk

Island and thence to New Zealand, where we
devoted ourselves to whaling in the Bay of Islands.
Whilst there, we nearly lost our ship in a skirmish
with the Maories, but we succeeded in getting
away with a full cargo and sailed for London,
taking with us two New Zealand natives named
Marquis and Teinah. Whilst rounding Cape Horn
we encountered a tremendous gale which compelled
us to run nearly 3,000 miles out of our course.
The delay thus occasioned made our provisions run
short, and we were obliged to steer for Otaheite,
the nearest place where we could conveniently lay
in a fresh supply. Although we obtained an abun-
dance of fresh meat in this beautiful island, a new
difficulty presented itself in the want of salt to
cure it. On this account we were detained two
months at the island manufacturing salt and curing
our meat. Our stock of sugar was also sadly
reduced, and we had to resort to the expedient of
squeezing the sugar-canes with the aid of a gun-
carriage and boiling down the juice to a syrup or
molasses, which proved a very satisfactory sub-
stitute.

I had thus a favourable opportunity of observing
the interesting people of Otaheite, whose manners

and customs have attracted so much attention from the civilised world. The females are remarkable for their stately and elegant persons, and they devote as much time and assiduity to the dressing of their hair and anointing it with oil as the finest ladies of London or Paris. The king was a native of the island of Ulitea, and like the old French monarchs and other great potentates had what might be termed his Swiss guards, consisting of 200 majestic-looking warriors collected from various islands, some even hailing from Peru. There is a remarkable similarity in the languages spoken by the natives of New Zealand, Otaheite, the Sandwich Islands and Peru, and even in the distinctions of rank and ceremony that are maintained in these widely scattered countries there is a remarkable resemblance. In Tongataboo there are no less than 22 castes or degrees of rank, "grades" as they would doubtless be called by the coiners of new tautological words, a species of counterfeit innovators whom I feel disposed to regard in the same light as I would the forgers of base money. A certain true and standard quality is as essential to distinguish the King's English as the King's money, and none else ought to be allowed to pass current.

Having at last procured a tolerable supply of provisions, we again set sail, taking with us, in addition to the two New Zealanders, a chief of Otaheite with a young companion of his. After rounding the Horn, our stock of biscuit became exhausted, and we had to fall back on the maize which we had shipped at Norfolk Island for the use of our pigs and poultry. It was therefore with very glad hearts we arrived on the coast of Brazil and cast anchor at St. Catherine's in a region of picturesque beauty. Here we remained three months refitting and repairing our ship, and we were detained for a similar period at St. Helena to wait for convoy, so it was not until June, 1806, that we arrived in London.

Being naturally desirous of visiting my native place after so long an absence, and being unwilling to leave the two New Zealanders and the two natives of Otaheite friendless in London, I introduced them to Sir Joseph Banks. He cheerfully took charge of them, defrayed all their expenses, and placed them under the care and tuition of the Rev. Joseph Hardcastle, in order that, by initiating them in the truths of the Christian religion, they might be able to confer a similar boon on their own countrymen when they returned to their native islands. Unfortunately, in little more than twelve months, the two Otaheitans died and also one of the New Zealanders. Only Marquis was proof against the rigours of the English climate, and he, being a tolerable carpenter, kept himself profitably employed.

On my return to Copenhagen, I found my native city bombarded by the English under Lord Cathcart. But I am unwilling to touch upon this painful episode, in which upwards of 1,500 of my country-men perished and a considerable portion of the best city in Europe was destroyed. The whole of the Danish fleet, that had previously been second only to that of England, was annihilated. The King of Denmark was then of necessity compelled to cast in his lot with Napoleon Buonaparte and was the last of his allies to abandon his cause.

Towards the close of this memorable year (1807) I was placed in command of a Danish vessel, armed with 28 small guns. My father and seven other merchants of Copenhagen, burning with a spirit of reprisal against the English, had subscribed together, purchased the vessel and presented it to the Crown. She was accordingly commissioned, manned, and

armed by the Government, and cutting through the
ice a month before it was expected that any vessel
could get out, we came unawares among the English
traders and captured eight or nine ships. This
success inspired me with fresh confidence, and
relying on my knowledge of the coast, I stood over
to England. I was in sight of Flamborough Head
when I discovered myself within reach of the *Sappho*
sloop of war, commanded by Captain Longford. A
little way beyond was another, which proved to be
the *Clio*, also British. I had no alternative, or time
for deliberation, neither indeed was any necessary.
My hopes of capturing others were all at once
changed into the one absorbing desire of saving
myself. I have frequently reflected that it is very
fortunate for man that the greatest and most trying
events of his life are generally of short duration,
often indeed but the work of a few moments. As
Dr. Johnson said when his master could not get him
to learn his lesson, he was flogged and there was
" an end on't." And in the same way when a
cannon-ball takes a man's head off, which he does
not expect, there's an end of him. The *Sappho* had
120 men and my vessel 83, but of course I had no
opportunity of making this calculation, or desire to

make it if I had, for we were speedily engaged.
We fought for three-quarters of an hour, and I
fired seventeen broadsides, but at last, my powder
being spent and my masts, rigging, and sails all
shot to pieces, I was under the necessity of doing
what many brave men have done before—to strike
my flag and surrender. Many of my men were
killed or wounded, but as a full account of the
engagement is recorded in the *London Gazette*, I
will not tire my readers with any further details of
it. Suffice it to say that Longford was made a
Post-Captain as a reward for the victory he obtained
over me on this occasion.

I was landed at Yarmouth, and on the following
day a letter was placed in my hands requesting me
to come to London to meet a public official connected with the Ministry, whose acquaintance I had
recently chanced to make near the British lines at
Copenhagen. Seeing my name in the newspapers,
he had sent a letter under cover to the Admiral of
the port, expressing his desire to see me. Through
him I became known to several of the high official
characters of that eventful period. Of course, as
soon as I arrived in London, I lost no time in paying my respects to Sir Joseph Banks. The

"SIR JOSEPH BANKS, THE FRIEND OF ART AND LETTERS,"

(*From the original drawing by J. Jorgenson, in the Egerton Collection at the British Museum.*)

benevolent feelings of that great and good man, in
unison with several other English gentlemen, were
at that time strongly interested in the fate of
Iceland.   The inhabitants of that remote island
were reduced almost to a state of famine owing to
the prohibition of the usual British supplies, which
was obstinately persisted in throughout the
hostilities carried on so fiercely between Denmark
and England.   Under these deplorable circumstances, permission was obtained from the British
Government to freight a ship with provisions for the
starving Icelanders, and I willingly agreed to take
command of her.   She was loaded at Liverpool,
and I sailed from that port on the 29th of
December, at a time when it was considered madness to attempt such a voyage, as, owing to the high
latitude of the country, the voyage would
necessarily have to be made at that season of the
year mostly in the dark.   But we found, as we
approached Iceland, that the hours of night were
brighter than those of day, so brilliant was the
reflection of the Northern Lights.   The insurance of
our vessel, though only 350 tons, cost 1,000
guineas, for it was considered a desperate enterprise.
Nevertheless, we arrived in perfect safety, and

5

experienced a most grateful welcome from the starving inhabitants. But the relief which one cargo could afford was far from sufficient, and I hastened back to Liverpool in order to bring out another.

CHAPTER III.

An Arbitrary Decree —No Trading with English Vessels—Arrest and
Deposition of the Danish Governor of Iceland—Jorgenson becomes
Monarch of the Island—The People Accept the Revolution —
Popular Reforms Initiated—A Tour of Iceland—A Rebellious
Prefect Subdued —Voyage to England—A Burning Ship—Arrival
in London—Arrested for Breaking Parole—Committed to Tothill
Fields Prison—Transferred to the Hulks—Liberated and Allowed
to Reside in Reading—Return to London—Enmeshed in the Wiles
of the Gambler—Reflections on a Ruinous Vice – Unpleasant
Voyage in a British Gunboat – Life in a Naval Hospital.

ON arriving at Liverpool, I lost no time in getting
to London and loading two more vessels with flour
and other provisions.   This time I had the pleasure
of taking with me, as passengers to Iceland, the
eminent botanist, Dr. Hooker, and Mr. Vancouver,
the brother of the famous voyager.   I was surprised
to discover on reaching the island that during my
absence a proclamation had been issued prohibiting
all communication with the English.   This had evidently been promulgated in order to prevent the
landing of my cargoes, for at the very time the
authorities were winking at the importation of a

5*

quantity of rye brought by a small Danish vessel,
which was sold to the people at the rate of forty-
shillings per 200 lbs. Of course I could not tamely
submit to such an arbitrary decree. I resolutely
refused to go back after a fruitless errand, and to
see a whole population deprived of the support
which Providence had brought to their doors in a
time of need. I formed my plan without taking
anyone into my confidence, and the day after my
arrival, being Sunday, I went on shore with 12 of my
sailors as soon as I saw that the people had gone to
church. I went straight to the Governor's house,
and dividing my little troop into two bodies, I
stationed six before and six behind the building,
with orders to fire upon anybody that should
attempt to interrupt me. I then opened the door
and walked in with a brace of pistols. His Lordship, Count Tramp, was reposing upon a sofa, all
unsuspicious of what was in progress, and was completely surprised by my abrupt appearance. With
the exception of the cook, who was busy preparing
dinner, one or two domestics, and a Danish lady, he
was alone in the house. Had he been religiously
disposed and gone to church with his people, I
would not have been able to effect my purpose so

easily. But as it happened, I had no difficulty
whatever in arresting the Count and escorting him
to a place of security on board my ship. I am not
aware, unless some more deeply-read historian than
myself can cite an instance, that any revolution in
the annals of nations was ever more adroitly, more
harmlessly or more decisively effected than this.
The whole government of the island was changed
in a moment without the firing of a shot or the
shedding of a drop of human blood. I was pretty
well aware of the sentiments of the people before I
planned my scheme, and had a shrewd suspicion
that all would be well ; nevertheless, to make
assurance doubly sure, I carefully secured the iron
chest of state. When the people emerged from
church they soon heard the news, and gathered in
astonished groups to discuss the arrest and deposition of their erstwhile governor, but feeling certain
that I would never have taken so bold and decisive
a step without the sanction and approval of the
British Government, they cheerfully submitted to
the new order of things and gradually dispersed to
their homes. Though I had not much practice in
this sort of business, I immediately issued a proclamation, in which I did not hesitate to announce

that the people of Iceland had thrown off the
intolerable yoke of the Danish oppression and had
unanimously called me to the head of the government.

Never was proclamation more successful. The
English inhabitants, supposing that I had concerted
the whole plot with the Icelanders on the occasion
of my first visit, never attempted to interfere, and
the resident Danes jumped to the conclusion that
I must have been supported in my *coup d'état*
both by the British and the Icelanders. All the
measures I adopted in my new character of monarch
of Iceland partook of the character of popular
reforms. I established trial by jury and free representative government. I relieved the people of
one-half of the taxes, making good the deficiency
of revenue by levying a small duty on the importation and the exportation of British goods, to
which I had thrown open the port. I augmented
the salaries of the clergy from the bishop down to
the humblest curate. Poor fellows! Some of the
pastors had not more than £12 a year to live upon,
and, in effecting so important a revolution, I could
not do less than raise their stipends to a more
decent and adequate scale. They were not wanting

in gratitude, for they all preached resignation and
contentment under the new order of things. I
advanced money for the benefit of public schools
and the fisheries, and compelled all public defaulters
to make up every deficiency from their private
estates. I released the people from all debts due to
the Crown of Denmark, which had so shamefully
withheld the subscriptions raised for the relief of
the Icelanders by the other European nations, but
especially by the English, after the dreadful
eruption of Hecla in 1783, when the island was
desolated by the overflow of lava. I erected a fort
of six guns to defend the harbour, raised a troop of
cavalry, and hoisted the ancient and independent
flag of Iceland, and I have the satisfaction of
knowing that the laws and regulations which I then
made remain for the most part in force and
undisturbed to this day.

When at Liverpool, I wrote to New York requesting that a ship might be sent to Iceland with
tobacco and other American produce, for, as the port
of Reikevig did not come within the operation of
the non-intercourse convention, it was freely open
to the ships of the United States. As the result of
my letter I had the pleasure of seeing a vessel enter

the harbour with a valuable cargo from New York,
which we received in exchange for British manufactures and other goods.

Having established my authority at headquarters, I found it advisable to make a tour of
the island. Though nearly destitute of trees,
Iceland is perhaps the most picturesque country in
the world, by reason of its great inequality of
surface and its ridges of precipitous mountains
capped with snow and ice. The main support of
the people is derived from sheep and the fisheries.
The wool of the Iceland sheep is coarse but strong,
and very useful. For seven or eight months of the
year the sheep require to be fed on hay. No grain
grows in the island, the climate being so cold that
in winter most of the houses have double doors and
windows. Strange to say, there are scarcely any
chimneys, the smoke being emitted through a hole
in the roof close to the gable and over the fireplace,
as in the huts of Scotland.

When I reached the house of the prefect or
magistrate of one of the northern districts, about
150 miles from Reikevig, he refused to acknowledge
my authority, or surrender the iron chest, but when
I ordered a quantity of brushwood to be placed

"INCIDENT AT AN ICELAND BALL."

(*From the original drawing by J. Jorgenson, in the Egerton Collection at the British Museum.*)

around his house, and when he saw I was determined
to set it on fire if he persisted in his opposition, he
changed his tone and submitted himself to my
jurisdiction.

Recognising the great advantages that would
accrue to Iceland if an amicable commercial treaty
could be arranged with England for the importation
of grain by licensed British vessels, I resolved to
visit London and endeavour to achieve this desirable
object. I took possession of a Danish ship that had
belonged to the deposed governor, Dr. Hooker and
the other passengers preferring to return by my own
vessel. We started away together, but I soon found
that the ex-governor's ship was by no means the
equal in sailing qualities to my old vessel. Fearing
that we should part company, I ran her between the
shore and the reef, a passage till then believed to be
impracticable. The other vessel went to leeward of
the reef, and, although I thus gained an advantage
of 17 miles on the wind, when daylight dawned we
saw our companion only three miles to leeward,
flying a signal of distress. We bore down upon her
in all haste and discovered that she had caught
fire, and that the flames were rapidly spreading.
General consternation prevailed on board the burning

vessel, and no systematic or effective efforts were being made either to extinguish the flames or save the lives of the people on board. I immediately ordered out the boats, and succeeded in bringing everyone safe on board our ship. Forgetting in the hurry and excitement of the scene that the guns of the burning vessel were loaded, we remained close to windward until three or four explosions in rapid succession warned us of our danger, and very nearly did us some damage. The firing of the guns by the intense heat, together with the flames blazing along the shrouds and sails, produced a striking effect upon the water, and when the hold and cargo caught fire—the latter consisting of wool, feathers, oil, tallow and tar — the spectacle was singularly and sublimely impressive. The copper bottom of my old ship continued to float on the surface of the sea like an immense burning cauldron long after the shades of night had descended on the scene. A breeze springing up, we were wafted away from the conflagration, but it continued in sight until we were fully 35 miles away. This catastrophe obliged us to return to Iceland for provisions. The passengers were put on board H.M.S. *Talbot,* which happened to be in the harbour at the time, and I again set sail for Liverpool, which I reached in eight days.

I lost no time in going up to London, and calling upon Sir Joseph Banks, but the *Talbot* had arrived before me, and her captain had falsely represented to the British Cabinet that I had established a Revolutionary Government in Iceland for the purpose of making that island a nest for all the dissatisfied persons in Europe. He furthermore reported that I was "highly unqualified to hold the command of a kingdom, because I had been an apprentice on board an English collier, and had served as a midshipman in an English man-of-war," alluding to the station I had occupied on board the *Lady Nelson.* Three weeks after my arrival, at about ten o'clock in the evening, as I was quietly taking some refreshment at my usual place of abode in London, the "Spread Eagle" in Gracechurch Street, I was arrested, and, next day, was brought before the Lord Mayor, charged with being an alien enemy, at large without the King's license, and with having broken my parole, although I had never given one.

I was sent to Tothill Fields prison, where I remained five weeks, and where I met with persons,

the effect of whose intimacy steeped my future life
in misery, in shades varied only by transient
glimpses of anticipation and remorse. Thence I
was transferred to a hulk set apart for the reception
of Danish prisoners, where I was kept in confinement for eleven months, after which, by the interest
of friends at Court, I was permitted to reside at
Reading, on my parole of honour. At this place I
occupied my time in the composition of a little
work entitled " The Copenhagen Expedition traced
to other causes than the treaty of Tilsit." After ten
months' residence at Reading I obtained permission
to employ myself as a British subject, and with that
intent made my way to London, but most unfortunately I was picked up in the metropolis by my
acquaintances of Tothill Fields prison, and was by
them initiated into all the enticements and horrors
of the gaming-table. For six months was I sunk in
this wretched vortex of dissipation, until at last I
found myself stripped of everything I had in the
world, including a sixteenth share of a £20,000
prize in a state lottery. Grave cause as I have seen
to reprobate the vice of drunkenness during the
manifold experiences of my chequered career, I am
compelled to denounce that of gambling, though

perhaps not so general, as a far more iniquitous and soul-absorbing propensity. The attacks of drunkenness are mainly in the first instance levelled at the body, but the demon of gambling lays siege at once to the citadel of the mind, and brings on the destruction of the body as a secondary consequence. When once this horrid vice has obtained possession of the heart, it absorbs and surmounts every other passion. The idea is ever present to the mind; it engrosses every thought. For ever expecting the vicissitude of success, the gamester goes on losing until all further hope of raising a stake is past. No cormorant or vampire ever contemplates the destruction of another so greedily as the gamester does that of his victim. They sit down together with the hope and determined savage purpose to devour each other, like the Irishman's two cats, till not a remnant of either be left. As for fair play or honesty, it is soon out of the question. The victim of sharpers resolves upon reprisal by becoming himself a sharper. It was not until after some months' experience that I discovered these men, with whom I had the misfortune to be seated at table, taking me by surprise when I thought (and thought rightly) that I had won, and coolly sweeping every shilling

off the table under my very eyes. Once or twice I
was bold enough to remonstrate, but I was instantly
silenced by a host of witnesses who were ready at
hand to contradict me.

Having been thus reduced to destitution, and
being filled with a desire at once to see the world
and to extricate myself from the charms of the
syren, I took my passage on board a vessel going
out to Lisbon. It so happened that Bellingham's
assassination of Mr. Perceval in the lobby of the
House of Commons was perpetrated just before our
vessel set sail, and I was the first to communicate the
unwelcome news to the British Consul. A suspicion
arose that I had spread the report from some
political motive, and as I could give no very satisfactory account of myself, and as it furthermore
appeared from some papers I had with me that I
had been a prisoner of war, I was arrested by order
of General Trant and sent back to England. Regaining my liberty, and being determined not to be
baulked in my purpose, I engaged as mate on a
merchant vessel, making an arrangement with the
captain to be discharged at Lisbon. Thence I
travelled through the lines and crossed the borders
of Spain. Returning to Lisbon, I again fell a prey

to my newly-acquired propensity for gambling, though I had lately suffered so much from it, and lost every shilling I had in the world. I sold the clothes I was wearing, and putting on a jacket and trousers, entered as a seaman in a gun-boat that was going home with the mail. Just as we were about starting the packet hove in sight, took our mails on board, and our gun-boat was despatched on a cruise off Cape St. Vincent.

Here we made prizes of several vessels, many of which, we found on examination, were furnished with false papers. On account of the ready and willing manner in which I performed my duty, I was soon placed in command of a watch, a promotion which excited some degree of jealousy against me among some of the officers. This ill-feeling increased to such an extent as to render my situation in the ship far from comfortable. On our going into Gibraltar, I was fortunate to get myself placed in the hospital, having gained the goodwill of the surgeon, to whom I took care to represent in its worst light an old complaint which sometimes troubled me. Thence I was sent home as an invalid, arriving at Portsmouth in 1813, and was placed on board the *Gladiator*, of 50 guns, which was stationed there to receive the invalids collected from the other ships in the Navy. Between 700 and 800 persons were packed into this horribly pent-up place, which could not have afforded even moderate accommodation for half that number, even if they had been in good health. As it was, the unfortunate invalids were obliged to remain on deck and below alternately night and day—a most trying experience, which occasioned the death of many. Altogether the situation was of the most distressing character, and the illness which I had been so anxious to magnify in order to get myself removed from the ship was now daily becoming serious, and I felt really and without exaggeration sick. Without reflecting whom I ought to address on the subject, I wrote a letter to the Admiral, representing the unsatisfactory condition of my health and requesting permission to go on shore. But in doing so I soon found I had taken a most imprudent step. The captain and the doctor, as soon as they heard of it, were both excessively angry and threatened to tie me up and flog me for " shamming Abraham," as the phrase is. I was now in a worse plight than ever, and felt really miserable. The captain in particular lost no opportunity of annoying me, frequently declaring that he would teach me to apply to the Admiral instead of to him, and that he was subject to the Lords of the Admiralty alone. Having failed in my first letter to the Admiral, I determined to try a second, for my situation could hardly be made worse than it was. I therefore wrote to the effect that I was exceedingly sorry I had given offence by addressing him on a former occasion through being unaware of the fact that the captain was subject to the Lords of the Admiralty, and not to him. The immediate consequence of this second letter was an order from the Admiral directing both the captain and myself to attend him on shore, when I had the pleasure of hearing the captain reprimanded and myself given liberty to go wherever I pleased.

CHAPTER IV.

I PROCEEDED to London, and, though clad merely in
jacket and trousers, was kindly received by some
friends of high rank and influence. After a brief
stay in the metropolis, I visited a much-esteemed
friend at his seat in Suffolk, who gave me a hearty
welcome. Availing myself of the quiet retirement
of his country residence, 1 secluded myself for a
time and wrote an account of the Icelandic revolution, which I presented to Sir Joseph Banks
One day, while I was busily engaged with my pen,
still clad as I was, in my sailor's garb, a gentleman
of high rank, who had come to visit my friend,
seeing me seated at the table with my papers
around me, inquired who that strange-looking man

was. "Oh," said my host, "allow me to introduce you to my friend the King of Iceland." We shook hands and engaged for some time in agreeable conversation. Having received pecuniary supplies from my friends in Copenhagen, and also had my funds replenished by some friends in England, to whom I had rendered some important services, I returned to London, where, I regret to say, I again yielded to my tempter, launched into extravagance, and made myself penniless once more.

At this time an important event of my life occurred. Amongst the acquaintanceships that I had formed during my confinement in Tothill Fields prison, was one with Count Dillon, a French cap· tive. Thinking me an enemy of England, and believing I had at that time been taken prisoner under circumstances similar to his own, one day, when he met me in a coffee-house in the Strand, he imparted to me a scheme which was then on foot, and had been concerted between the Americans and the French, with the object of sending out an armed expedition to take possession of the Australian colonies. The idea had originated in the reports which had been sent in by the French navigator, Captain Baudin, of the *Geographe*, who

6*

had visited Australia in 1801. At that time I
had the pleasure of seeing him in Sydney. He was
a man intensely anxious to distinguish himself by
doing something that no man before him had ever
accomplished. On the occasion of his making an
exploring tour into the interior of New South Wales
I was induced to accompany him, and all his
ambition was to advance further than any Englishman had ever been before. We had travelled about
100 miles from Sydney, and had ascended a considerable distance up the Hawkesbury, some marked
tree or remains of a temporary hut giving constant
indication that a European had been there at some
previous period. I had become very impatient at
his incessant reasons, thus continually discovered,
for penetrating farther, with so futile an object as
that of returning to Paris and boasting that he had
been where no other traveller had stood before him.
So, spying a large white rock projecting from an
eminence ahead, I ran forward and, standing upon
it, cried out with a show of exultation that that was
the point beyond which no white man had ever
penetrated. Baudin then marched about twenty
paces farther, and returned with his ambition fully
satisfied.

I may here take the opportunity to mention in
this connection, what I omitted to record in its
proper place, that Captain Flinders, when his ship,
the *Investigator*, had been condemned, after the
circumnavigation of Australia, transferred himself
and his crew to the *Porpoise* man-of-war, which
was unfortunately wrecked upon a reef in Torres
Straits, in the attempt to proceed to India by that
dangerous route.   Captain Flinders voyaged all the
way to Sydney in an open boat, to obtain succour for
his shipwrecked companions, and succeeded in his
heroic mission.   He resumed his homeward voyage
in a small craft, called the *Cumberland*, that had
been placed at his command by the Governor of
New South Wales. It is painful, and even heart-
rending to me to recite the distressing details of
the subsequent misfortunes of my old commander,
that most indefatigable explorer of these Australian
coasts, to whom posterity will ever owe a heavy
debt of gratitude.   Running short of provisions and
relying on his passport, which, by the general
consent of civilised nations, gave free access and
egress to discovery ships, whether in an enemy's
port or not, Captain Flinders steered the *Cumberland* to the Mauritius, at that time a French

colony, where he was detained under suspicion of being a spy by the French Governor, who refused to believe that an officer of his rank in the British Navy would be sailing in so small a vessel as the *Cumberland.* At least that was the ostensible reason assigned, but it has been conjectured, inasmuch as his charts and papers were never more heard of, that the French were hastening, in the meantime, to publish and profit by his discoveries, in connection with those made by their own navigator, Baudin, to whom I have just referred. Captain Flinders was kept a prisoner in the Mauritius for nearly seven years, until liberated by the peremptory orders of Napoleon, but the intrepid navigator did not long survive his release and his return to England.

The fate of his companion, Dr. Bass, was more tragic still. After completing the survey of the northern part of the straits that bear his name, he proceeded to England, but soon returned to the Antipodes with Captain Bishop, as supercargo and part owner of the brig *Venus,* loaded with a cargo intended partly for Sydney and partly for the Spanish settlements in South America. At Sydney Captain Bishop became insane, and the command of the ship devolved upon Dr. Bass, who was a skilful navigator as well as a surgeon and physician. He proceeded to Valparaiso and proposed to the authorities of that port what was common enough at that troublous time, the alternative of "forced trade"—in other words, "Buy my goods or I'll open fire on the town." The Spanish Americans professed to comply, and gave him permission to trade, but when Dr. Bass and a considerable portion of his crew went unguardedly on shore, imprudently relying for safety on the consent that had been given, the vessel and cargo were seized, Dr. Bass and his people were taken prisoners, sent to the quicksilver mines, and never heard of again. The working of these horrible mines is indeed certain death in a very few years to the unfortunate creatures condemned to it, for the mineral so pervades the system that they cannot remain above ground again without suffering dreadful attacks of cold, fever, and shivering ague.

Dr. Bass was not the only daring trader who was consigned to this frightful doom. About the same time Captain McClarence, of the *Dart*, sailed from Sydney on a similar expedition, and met, with all his crew, a like fate at the port of Coquimbo.

Captain Campbell, of the *Harrington*, had better
luck.   During the short peace of Amiens, this bold
adventurous man, shrewdly calculating on the
speedy renewal of the war, sailed from Sydney to
Spanish America, entered several of its ports,
plundered the houses of many of the wealthiest
inhabitants and even despoiled many of the
churches.   He returned to Australia with an
immense treasure, but being doubtful of the
reception that awaited him at the hands of the
Governor in Sydney, he took the precaution of
burying a large portion of it on one of the most
unfrequented islands of the Straits.   His doubts
proved to be well founded, for Governor King placed
him and all his crew under arrest, and they were
kept under detention until news of the recommence-
ment of hostilities arrived.   The smart, long-headed
captain was then able to show that he had collected
his booty subsequent to the declaration of
war, although he had no actual knowledge of
the fact.   These singular events and many others
of the like character that came under my observation attracted little notice at a time when
the interest and attention of the world were
concentrated on the contentions of the Euro-

pean nations, and the mighty campaigns of
Napoleon.

But to return from this digression to the projected invasion of the Australian colonies by the
combined French and Americans. As told to me by
Count Dillon at our interview in London, the plan
concerted between the French and the Americans
was that each should provide two armed vessels to
meet at a certain rendezvous, sail away in company
and participate in the plunder obtained from the
Australian colonies. From my long sojourn and
intimacy with the English and the many kindnesses
I had experienced from English gentlemen high in
position and power, I did not feel disposed to keep
silence on the subject of such a deep-laid plot
against a remote dependency of the British Crown,
to which by long residence I had in a certain
measure become endeared. I lost no time, therefore, in communicating what I had heard to a friend
connected with the Colonial Office. But when
an official of high station in that department was
informed of it, he looked upon the scheme as so wild
and so unlikely to be carried into effect at a time
when the whole energies of Europe were drawn to
a vortex in the life-and-death continental struggle,

that he totally disregarded my information, saying
to my friend :—" There is no fear. The attempt is
not worth their while, and even if they did make it
and succeed, England would lose little or nothing.
These colonies are not worth keeping, for they
already cost us £100,000 a year."

Nothing therefore was done by the British
Government to intercept the expedition and save
Australia from foreign domination, but Providence
interposed to avert that calamity. The two French
ships under Count Dillon were overtaken by a
violent storm and wrecked near Cadiz, and that put
an end to the enterprise as far as France was concerned. Not so with the Americans, who, though
bereft of the assistance of their allies, proceeded out
to Australian waters, where they captured and burnt
no less than seventeen of our whaling ships. This
happened in the memorable year 1813, when, owing
to the deficiency thus created in the London
market, sperm oil rose to an enormous price. It is
much to be regretted that the navigation, fisheries,
and trade of these southern seas should have been
so long overlooked by the authorities at home. The
immense archipelago of the Pacific is inhabited by
thousands of friendly-disposed people ready and

anxious to exchange their commodities for British manufactures. The benign influence of the Christian religion, which is rapidly spreading through the efforts of our evangelistic missionaries, is doing much to raise these people in the scale of civilisation, and, although the activity of the Americans is hourly taking advantage of our comparative supineness, nevertheless, the approach of the British flag is always hailed with superior satisfaction. The pearl fisheries are said to be more profitable and less hazardous than the pursuit of the sperm whale, and the sandalwood and *béche-de-mer*, which are produced so abundantly on the northern coasts of Australia, are known to yield the Dutch, through the medium of the Malays, an immense revenue. Nothing surprised Captain Flinders more, when voyaging in these latitudes, than the immense fleets of Malay prows actively engaged in this traffic, which he encountered in the Gulf of Carpentaria on the north of Australia.

My provoking propensity for gambling continued to assail me at this time, and, in defiance of my sober judgment and repeated losses, I persisted in it until my career as a gamester was summarily cut short by my being arrested for debt and committed

to the Fleet prison, where I was confined for two
years. When the news of the capture and
destruction of the British whaling vessels in the
South Seas was sent home, I did not fail to write to
the Colonial Minister, regretting that the information I had given of the project when it might have
been nipped in the bud had been disregarded.
This communication proved to have been very
wisely conceived and was the means of procuring
me friends of influence, whose kindness I long continued to experience. I was now permitted to
enjoy the Rules of the prison, and having been so
fortunate as to reimburse my funds I was weak
enough to launch forth again into the vortex of
gambling. The passion was so overpowering that I
exceeded the limits of the Rules in order to play at
a notorious gaming table in the West-end of
London. One day I had the misfortune, as I was
entering the door of the gaming-house, to come
full-butt upon the clerk of the prison, who, I felt
certain, would inform against me. My resolution
was immediately taken, for I had acquired some
experience in the art of circumventing. I ran back
as fast as I could and, entering the public coffee-
room of the prison, made a noise as if by accident,

so as to attract attention, looking at the clock at the same time and exclaiming the hour as if in surprise to find it was so late. It was a very important consideration for me, as a violator of the Rules could never after be entitled to enjoy that privilege or the benefit of the Insolvent Act, for which I was desirous of applying. However, I did not suffer for my imprudence, and my friends at last came forward and furnished me with money to pay my debt. The reader will hardly believe, for I can scarcely believe it myself, that instead of doing so and getting myself liberated, the hold that the gaming table had upon me was so inveterate that I returned to it and lost every penny.

I was now completely locked up in prison, and in order to divert my unpleasant reflections on my own folly and the more to reconcile myself to my fate, I went vigorously to work on the writing of a romantic episode in the history of Afghanistan, with the particulars of which I had become intimately acquainted. I also composed during my confinement a tragedy suggested by the cruel execution of the Duc D'Enghein by order of Napoleon, an event which at that time was exciting considerable public sympathy. A statistical essay

on the Russian Empire was another work on which
I employed myself at this period. I made several
neatly-written copies of these compositions, and
presented them to different noblemen and gentlemen
of whom I had some knowledge, and who rewarded
me very handsomely for my pains.

I now began to seriously reflect and to entertain
the cheering hope that I had attained sufficient
firmness to withstand any further attacks of my
inveterate vice. It was whilst thus congratulating
myself on having thoroughly subdued the one
enemy of my peace, prosperity and happiness, that
I was visited one afternoon by a Government
messenger, bearing a letter from a gentleman
holding a high position in the Foreign Office
requesting me to call upon him. I did so, and our
interview resulted in my being engaged on a
diplomatic mission to the seat of war, the debt
for which I was imprisoned was immediately discharged, I was provided with sufficient funds to
enable me to proceed abroad, and was given permission when on the Continent to draw upon London
for all reasonable expenses of travelling. It seems
incredible, but it is literally true that, notwithstanding this unexpected stroke of good luck, in

spite of all my self-congratulations on having finally
conquered the enemy, I surrendered myself once
more to the demon of my life, and so desperate was
I in my gambling pursuit—unfortunate as I almost
invariably was—that I not only lost all the money
that had been advanced to me for the purposes of
my journey, but actually risked and forfeited the
very clothes with which I had provided myself to
go abroad. When I could no longer raise a shilling
to throw away on the gaming-table and was totally
destitute of the means of living in London, my
remorse and vexation of spirit were indescribably
bitter. Of course it was out of the question to
apply again to my principals at the Foreign Office,
who would naturally conclude that I had reached
the Continent long before, and whom I would now
be ashamed to meet. What I did in the
emergency was to exchange the garb I was wearing
with an old-clothes man in return for a sailor's
jacket and trousers. Thus arrayed, I proceeded to
Gravesend, where I represented myself to the
master of a transport going over with stores as
belonging to a vessel which had left me behind, and
which I was desirous of rejoining at Antwerp. By
this means I succeeded in getting to Ostend, where

I could replenish my empty purse by exercising the privilege granted me of drawing on London. But on producing my letter of credit, a new and startling difficulty unexpectedly arose, for my sailor's dress was so inconsistent with the appearance which my application led the bankers to expect, that I was looked upon as an impostor. I was in despair over this annoying and most embarrassing discomfiture, not knowing how in the world to overcome the difficulty when, by a lucky accident, I met an officer of the British Army to whom I was personally known, and who forthwith testified to my identity.

CHAPTER V.

I WAS now in a position to assume an appearance more respectable and more in harmony with the character of the duty I had undertaken. I proceeded to Ghent, and I had not been there three days when it became evident that Waterloo was the point at which the epoch-making blow that was to decide the fate of Europe, would be struck. I hastened on, and was a silent spectator of those memorable events that followed in rapid succession from the 16th to the 18th of June, 1815, and which culminated in the precipitate flight of Napoleon and the final overthrow of his once-mighty power. I will not attempt to describe the amazing panorama of the field of Waterloo. This

7

has already been done by many able pens. Keeping to my personal narrative, suffice it to say that I went with the fugitive stream to Paris, where 400,000 fighting men had soon collected after the catastrophe of Waterloo. The London Foreign Office gentleman who had engaged my services met me in Paris by appointment, and under his directions I was engaged for some time in delicate diplomatic business that brought me into contact with several of the most celebrated men of that day. In particular, I had the pleasure of forming an acquaintance with a French General, who was a great favourite of Napoleon, and is now a Marshal of France.

My diplomatic work in Paris having been brought to a satisfactory close, my employer entered into a fresh engagement with me to proceed to Warsaw, from which I was to communicate with him. He replenished my pocket liberally as before, to defray my travelling expenses on the journey. But 1 could not quit the gay metropolis of France, without witnessing for once the science of the gaming-table as practised in its highest perfection. I went at first with no intention whatever of playing, but simply as a spectator. Alas! the temptation was once more too strong for me. I hazarded a stake, and, I may say unfortunately, was at first a winner, for my luck soon turned and I continued to be a loser for several subsequent nights. My principal was in Paris all this time under the impression that I had started on my journey. On the last occasion in London, as the reader will remember, I retained my clothes when I had lost all my money, but in Paris I played so desperately that I had actually to sell my shirt to a sergeant for seven francs, in the cold month of December, and, buttoning up my coat, set out on foot on the north road at the east gate of Paris.

Observing the strictest economy and putting up with every possible privation, I contrived to get as far as the little town of Joncherie, about 120 miles from Paris, where I was reduced to my last sou. But I had lived long enough to learn not to starve in a Christian country. Seeing the door of a little cabaret or ale-house standing open, I walked boldly in, and, although I had nothing in my pocket, I assumed the boldest face I could, and called for a good dinner, as if I had plenty of money. As I was enjoying my banquet, the mayor of the place, who happened to be a Bourbonist, called to see my

7*

passport. In taking it out of my pocket, I purposely pulled a letter along with it, which I dropped upon the floor in order that he might pick it up.

"Do you know the hand-writing on the back of that letter," I enquired.

He replied in the negative.

I then showed him that it was from the Duchess of Angoulème, a circumstance that I knew from the bias of his politics would serve to materially ingratiate me into his favour. I further told him that I was an Irishman going on a pilgrimage to the Holy Land.

"Then," said he, "you must not leave the village without seeing our excellent lady, the Baroness D'Este, who I am sure will be very glad to receive any person going on such a pious mission."

I waited on the Baroness, and had the good fortune to find that my poverty was rather a recommendation than otherwise. She readily paid all my expenses at the inn, and gave me besides several coins to take with me and deposit at the sacred shrine. Her reception of me was so kind that I remained ten days, and formed an acquaintance with the Cure, a good, unassuming country pastor, possessed of no small share of learning and general intelligence.

With this very opportune aid I was able to continue my journey as far as Rheims. The politics of this ancient city, I found, were diametrically opposed to those of my last resting-place. The prefect was a zealous Bonapartist, and I contrived to secure an introduction, which I improved with such assiduity and success that he not only furnished me with a supply of money, but gave me a billet which entitled me to a certain sum per mile to defray my expenses on the road, besides the supply of a horse to carry me from station to station. At one of these villages the mayor, a blustering suspicious sort of man, after surveying me from head to foot, refused to renew my billet for the horse, saying I was a lazy fellow and able enough to walk. I was provoked and irritated by his taunting expressions and supercilious behaviour, and, suddenly clenching my fist, I gave him a tolerably effective thump on the head. A loud outcry immediately ensued and the villagers came forth in crowds, armed with pitchforks and other weapons, the sight of which

convinced me that I had better take to my heels
forthwith.

I managed to get as far as Metz, where a kind of
low Dutch is spoken. On paying my respects to the
mayor, I soon found by his abortive attempts to
speak it, that he could not read French very well,
the language in which my billet was written. A
little ready presence of mind is necessary for most
men to avoid being thrown back upon the world, and
I have on almost all occasions, both in the old
world and the new, found that a certain degree of
modest assurance is a great help to a man in
getting through life. So placing my billet in the
mayor's hand, without giving him the slightest
inkling of my belief in his inability to read it, I
said, "You will see, sir, by that document, with
what you are to supply me."

He looked at it with a profound assumption of
knowledge and authority, assented with the utmost
gravity, and ordered that I should have everything
I required. With the help thus afforded, I arrived
at the frontier, where I had the satisfaction of
having my billet again renewed. After 22 days'
easy travelling, I arrived at Frankfort. It was a
very rainy day, and I entered the town miserably

drenched, and not knowing what to do. Seeing me roaming aimlessly about, and staring at the shops, a Jew came up, under the impression that I was one of his brethren from Poland, come to visit the fair, but when I related my story to him, he abruptly turned away and left me. Recollecting the old proverb, which though it could hardly have been uttered by so honest a man as Solomon, struck me at the time as being tolerably correct, namely, "that a man might as well be hanged for a sheep as a lamb," I entered a good inn, ordered a sumptuous meal, and went to bed.

At breakfast the next morning I sent for the landlord and told him very frankly that I had no money, that he must wait a little, as I should have some in the course of the day. And, truth to tell, I had already, on so many occasions, been unexpectedly supplied with the means of sustenance and travel, that I flattered myself fortune would once more prove propitious before the day was over, in such a place as Frankfort. Walking through the town, my eye caught the name of Fraser, a celebrated mathematical instrument maker, and a Scotchman. On entering his shop I found that he had a chronometer of my father's making,.

which served to introduce me. He was a most humane and amiable man, and gave me his best advice. He showed me the way to the house of Lord Clancarty, the British minister. I proceeded there, and sent in my name. My shabby attire attracted the unfavourable notice of the servants, who came and peeped at me in evident suspicion, as if they fancied I was an assassin meditating the murder of his lordship. I was in this uncomfortable position, standing on the tip-toe of suspense, when a side-door opened, and a gentleman attached to the Foreign Office, whom I had the pleasure of knowing, came out and recognised me. This providential meeting led to a removal of all my pecuniary difficulties.

On my departure from Frankfort, Mr. Fraser kindly gave me an introduction to the secretary of the Grand Duke of Hesse-Darmstadt. On presenting it, I had the pleasure of being introduced to His Highness, with whom I had some very interesting conversation regarding what I had seen in the Australian colonies, for the Duke was a learned and a scientific man. I spent some hours in looking over his museum, which comprised an immense collction of natural curiosities and fossil remains. His gallery of paintings was certainly one of the finest in Europe. On taking my leave, His Highness made me a handsome present.

Saxe-Weimar was my next stopping-place, and there I had the high honour of being introduced to the venerable Goethe. I met him in the library of the Duke, a magnificent collection of upwards of 200,000 volumes. Goethe was a member of the Privy Council, besides filling the office of librarian to the Duke, a situation, needless to say, far more congenial to his literary tastes and habits. Though growing old at this time, the illustrious dramatic poet, the Shakespeare of Germany, was as full of life and spirits as a young student. He wore the dress of a privy councillor—a blue coat with gold facings. In appearance Goethe was somewhat portly, rather tall, with hazel eyes, remarkably heavy eye-brows, and a dark complexion.

My recruited funds enabled me to hire a carriage now, and travel with some degree of state to Berlin. There I visited, not only the British Minister, but my distinguished countrymen, Niebuhr and Bernstorf; the former was at the head of the finance department, and the latter was minister for foreign affairs, and a man of great political tact. I remained

in Berlin for seven or eight months, procrastinating
from day to day my departure for Warsaw. For I
had here the good or rather the bad fortune to gain
a prize of 400 crowns in the Prussian lottery, in
which a ticket could be bought for three English
shillings. This incident revived the slumbering
passion within me, and I gave myself up once more
to every excess of gambling. I was more fortunate
on this than on any former occasion in which I embarked in play. My companions were strictly
honourable, for the fraternity of sharpers is
mostly confined to the hells, as they are aptly called,
of London and Paris. But the propensity to play
in Berlin, as well as in most other towns on the
Continent, is very great indeed. The gamblers
commence their whist in the coffee-houses in the
middle of the day, and, votary to the syren as I
was myself, I could not help reflecting what a
large portion of the best period of their lives was
thrown away in so useless, inane and unsatisfactory
a pursuit.

During my stay at Berlin I visited the celebrated
residence of Frederic II., Sans Souci, near Potsdam,
about twenty miles from Berlin. The building,
though large, had a comfortable cottage appearance.

So general was the respect for the old King that, during all the bitter contests of the time, Napoleon would not suffer the structure to be disturbed in the least particular. A sword was indeed once taken from the palace to Paris, but was subsequently restored. I spent some time looking over the library, and came upon a fine edition of Voltaire. The miller, his family, and the historic mill in the middle of the garden were still undisturbed. Frederic, being desirous of removing the mill from the garden, went one day to the miller (the father of the one I saw), with an intimation that he must sell it, and betake himself elsewhere. But the miller politely, but firmly, declined the royal request. " What, Sir," exclaimed the King in a passion, " don't you know who I am, and that I could take it from you, if I liked, whether you will or no ? " " Yes, I dare say you would, please your majesty," replied the miller, " if there was no Supreme Court in Berlin to prevent you." Frederic instantaneously cooled down, and was so pleased with this manly, straightforward answer, that he contented himself with asking the man to permit him to repair the mill at his own expense, so that it might no longer remain an ugly eye-sore in the middle of his pleasure-ground. To this proposal the miller, of course, cheerfully assented. His son, however, having a large family, was constrained to request William, the present King, to buy the mill, in order to provide means for his children. But the King very handsomely replied, that he could not think of buying the mill, as it was now identified with the history of Prussia, but he hoped the enclosed 6,000 crowns would serve the purpose equally well. Not far from. Sans Souci stands a stupendous palace, built by Frederic II., at an expense of three millions sterling, but never occupied by any of the Royal family. When I went to pay it a visit, I found only one porter at the lodge, an old veteran. As I came up to make some inquiries about the building, he was pouring some clear liquid out of a bottle into a tumbler, which he swallowed at a draught. I ventured to remark that I would feel grateful for a glass of water also, whereupon he suddenly assumed an expression of the utmost indignation. " That's not water," he cried, " it's good corn-brandy. Water is only fit for dogs to drink."

I must not omit to mention here the interviews I had at Berlin with the now celebrated traveller,

Prince Puckler Von Muskaw, then a Count. He
had formerly been Minister Plenipotentiary to the
Court of St. James's from the Saxon King, but, by
the dismemberment of Saxony, the province in
which the Count's estate was situated became subject to Prussia. He certainly possessed great
abilities and courted notoriety, though rather eccentric in his ways of pursuing it. When I was at
Berlin he made a balloon ascent, in company with a
female aeronaut, to whom he made a present of
500 crowns. On another occasion he was so well
pleased with the performance of an actress in the
Berlin Theatre, which is one of the handsomest in
Europe, that he presented her next day with a
diamond necklace of great value. His entertain-
ments to the King, Royal family and Ministers were
always on the most splendid scale. His writings,
though very sarcastic in parts, have served to
expose many of the fashionable vagaries of the
English.

Amongst other gambling associates in Berlin, I
had several times the satisfaction of playing with
old Marshal Blucher, who was passionately fond of
his pipe and a game at whist. I frequently visited
the library of the old Marshal Prince Henry, uncle

to the present king, and had several conversations on the literature of the day with the librarian, the Rev. W. Beresford, one of those who were obliged to leave England when the famous Corresponding Society was broken up. At the time of my visit, the King of Prussia did not reside in the Royal Palace of Berlin, but lived in a plain house in the city, so as to avoid the glare, the ceremony, and the expense of a large establishment. In the sleeping apartments of the young princesses, one of whom is now an Empress, I observed three little tent-bedsteads without curtains.

I should have been more uneasy and even ashamed at dallying so long in Berlin without fulfilling the main object of my mission at Warsaw, had I not been so fortunate as to form an acquaintance with some Poles, from whom I collected much of the information that it was my duty to obtain. The facts and particulars thus acquired I embodied in a despatch to my principals. At last I tore myself away from the allurements of the Prussian capital, and set out for Dresden in the month of November, 1816. The good fortune which had attended me in Berlin now deserted me, and I had not been in Dresden two days when I fell among sharpers, and was completely fleeced. I was actually so senselessly imprudent as to sit down and lose £500 with a fellow whom I knew to be disreputable and not worth ten shillings. The abominable set in which I got mixed up at this place so thoroughly ruined me that I began to lose my usual flow of spirits, which on all former occasions had supported me in my reverses. Seeing several hundred miles before me in the depth of winter, I gave up all idea of proceeding to Warsaw and resolved to return to London. I was obliged to dispose of all my equipment, except the clothes I was wearing, for a few pounds to assist me on the road. I was afraid that my sharping acquaintances, if they suspected my intention, would take steps to detain me on account of some alleged debts which they pretended I owed, and I therefore considered it most expedient to get away without applying for a passport. But the want of this useful document subjected me to no small inconvenience and put my ingenuity very frequently to the rack. Being on foot, however, I was less suspected, and could often make my way into the towns of an evening, or out of them in the morning, by walking boldly and unconcernedly past the gate, as if I belonged to the

place or to the countrymen in the vicinity coming in
with their farm produce.

I recall one evening in particular when the man
at the gate of a small fortified town peremptorily
refused to let me pass unless I could produce my
passport. I was fatigued and hungry after my long
walk. My earnest entreaties and the noise of our
altercation at last brought out the gatekeeper's wife
to see what was the matter. Approaching her, I
pulled out two silk handkerchiefs which I had in
my pocket, and begged her to intercede on my
behalf, for it would be my ruin to be shut out that
night, as I was hourly expecting my cart with a load
of smuggled goods, which would stand a great
chance of being seized if I were not at hand to
receive it, at the same time requesting her accept-
ance of the best of the two handkerchiefs, and
promising her some very advantageous bargains
when the goods came up. The effect of this little
invention soon operated in my favour. I was invited
to supper at the gate-house, and was comfortably
lodged there for the night. After a hearty breakfast in the morning, affecting surprise that my cart
had not yet come up, I said I would move on a few
steps to look after it, and so proceeded on my journey.

Much as I had failed in examining and reforming the passions of my own heart, the various vicissitudes of my life had led me to regard minutely the workings of human nature in the breasts of others. For instance, considerable reluctance was often shown to disclose to me the different points of information which it was my duty from time to time to obtain. With some a certain amount of flattéry and prudently applied commendation would succeed in drawing the cat out of the bag. Others would present themselves before me firmly resolved to reveal nothing. A different policy was of course necessary in the case of persons of such determined silence.

" Pooh," I would say to a man of this type, " you pretend to know all about this. Why, you know nothing at all about the matter. I know more about it myself than you do."

Bristling up at once, he would perhaps clench his fist in my face, saying :

" Don't I know anything about it, though ? "

Then I would lead him on from one step to another, until at last I had extracted from him everything I wanted.

CHAPTER VI.

A Baffled Emigration Project—Three Years of London Gambling
—A Saddening Sequel—In Newgate Prison—Appointed Hospital
Assistant—Impressions and Experiences—Newgate, a Gigantic
School of Vice—Indecent Rapidity of Trials—The Strange Story
of a Bank of England Clerk.

ON my return to London I had, notwithstanding all
my shortcomings and discrepancies, the satisfaction
to be well received by my principals of the Foreign
Office, and to be handsomely rewarded for the duties
I had performed. With the money thus acquired I
had resolved to emigrate to Spanish America, which
at that time offered a favourable field for persons of
my adventurous disposition. Still deluded, however, by the false hopes that the gaming-table so
incessantly held out to me, I ventured a small stake
in the expectation of adding to the little fund
which I had collected to take with me. But once
within the magic circle I was wholly unable to get
out, and instead of carrying my emigration project
into effect, I spent the next three years of my life

(from 1817 to 1820) in a continual whirl of misery
and disappointment at the gaming-table. I look
back upon this dark period of my chequered career
with the deepest regret, and would, if I could, blot
it out entirely from the records of my existence.
The final and pitiful result of these three years of un-
bridled folly and disheartening dissipation was that,
through the ingratitude and low cunning of a person
who resided with me in Tottenham Court Road I
was arrested one day on a charge of having pawned
certain articles of furniture belonging to my landlady. The case was tried at the Old Bailey, and I
had the mortification to be sentenced to seven
years' transportation. But instead of being sent
out to the penal settlements in these colonies, I was
placed under the surgeon of Newgate Prison, the
late Dr. Box, as an assistant in the hospital. I continued to hold this appointment for twenty months,
until, in consequence of the satisfaction I had given
the doctor, and the favourable notice of the sheriffs,
my case was more minutely examined, and on its
appearing that the articles for the loss of which I
had been sentenced had been actually pawned in
the name of my fellow-lodger, and not in mine, I
had the pleasure to obtain my pardon under the

8*

condition that I should quit the kingdom within a month from the day of my liberation.

Some of my impressions and experiences during my stay in Newgate may be worth placing on record. There was a very proper regulation providing that no female visitors should be allowed to enter the prison, save such as were married. One consequence of it, however, was that many single prisoners, in order to obtain interviews with their former female associates, declared themselves married, never thinking of the awkward consequences of such a confession to themselves after they were transported to a new country. For their declarations were of course recorded against them in the books of the gaol and transmitted in the lists sent along with them to the penal settlements of Australia and Van Diemen's Land. But the great majority of the prisoners in Newgate were persons awaiting their trials, and as no work was required of them, by reason of the idleness thus induced and the mixture of the different characters and shades of criminality, the place was literally a gigantic school of vice. Cards, though prohibited by the regulations, were smuggled in in spite of the keepers, and were continually being played, in addition to other games of chance with which I had already become familiarised during my imprisonment at Tothill Fields. In my capacity of assistant to the surgeon, I was enabled to ascertain pretty intimately the characters and particulars of the cases of all who entered Newgate, and, although I have often heard people affirm the contrary, I can safely say that of all who were committed to prison during my time not one was an innocent person. Of course I speak of crimes and misdemeanours, not of those who were imprisoned for the non-payment of fines. There were always several of this latter class under detention. Whilst I was in Newgate, a nobleman of high rank, now holding a prominent office in one of the colonies, suffered an imprisonment of twelve months and paid a fine of £5,000 to the Crown.

Among the prisoners who particularly attracted my notice was the captain of a slave-ship, who had been captured whilst trafficking at Madagascar, in a vessel belonging to the Mauritius. He was tried for the offence in the Admiralty Court, and sentenced to 14 years' transportation. He had visited the court of Radama, the late king of Madagascar, and had made a series of interesting notes, which I assisted him in arranging and trans-

lating into English. They embodied many interesting particulars of that fine island. Amongst
other facts it was stated that considerable traffic
was carried on with the continent of Africa by an
ancient colony of about 4,000 Arabs, who were
settled on the west coast of Madagascar. Many of
the inhabitants were described as persons of
considerable intelligence, and the reigning queen
was said to encourage intercourse with the English
—an enlightened policy that might gradually lead
to the systematic development of the resources of
Madagascar and to commercial relations with the
Australian colonies, as well as with the Mauritius
and Europe.

The great, and I might almost add the indecent
rapidity with which many of the trials at the Old
Bailey were conducted, has been referred to by the
able author of " The Schoolmaster in Newgate."
At the same time it cannot be denied that many of
the oldest and wiliest of the prisoners serve by
their own conduct to accentuate the short average
time occupied by each case in court. These men,
who have perhaps been tried before for offences at
this tribunal, are already well aware of the probable
result, and know that if they give the Court much

trouble and prolong by an ineffectual defence the period of their trial, they will, in all probability, be prolonging also the period of their punishment. I well remember one day when five men were arraigned at the bar. The four who were most guilty, on being asked their plea by the Court, answered promptly, with much seeming contrition, " Guilty, my lord," and were let off with a few months' imprisonment, whilst the fifth, being sensible of his comparative innocence, pleaded " Not guilty," occupied the time of the Court with his defence for three-quarters-of-an-hour, and was sentenced to seven years' transportation.

Money, which, until proved otherwise, it is reasonable to conclude has been honestly acquired, always, in a civilised community, draws a degree of respect which will induce even Courts of Justice to treat an accused party with every possible fairness and calm deliberation. A remarkable instance of this occurred whilst I was at Newgate, in the case of one of the principal clerks of the Transfer-office of the Bank of England. He was committed on a charge of having used the means which his confidential employment afforded him, to make away, either by embezzlement or

forgery, with a large amount of stock standing in
the name of the late Sir Robert Peel. The pre-
sumptive evidence against him was very strong.
When a suspicious discovery was made, he absented
himself from the bank ; several brokers swore to his
having ordered the stock to be sold out in eight
different shares, and £4,000 of the money paid by
the brokers were found in his possession. So
sensible did he appear to be of his own guilt, and of
the certainty of his fate if put upon his trial, that
when he was apprehended, he attempted to escape
from the bed-room in the third story of the house
where the police officer, under whose charge he was,
had locked him up for the night. He had made a
rope of the sheets of his bed to let himself down,
but he imprudently descended with his hands only,
and not as the sailors do, holding on by the legs
also, and thus slipping down steadily. From not
attending to this precaution, the rope swayed
alternately to and fro, and threw him against the
window of the room beneath, in which his captor
slept. This so alarmed him that he let go his hold
and fell into the street, fracturing his jaw-bone, one
of his hip-bones, and one of his arms.

In this deplorable condition he was conveyed to

Newgate, and so desperate did his case appear that
every precaution was taken lest he should do himself some personal violence in order to avoid the
ignominy of a public trial and execution. His
amiable wife attended him with unwearied assiduity
and affection, and as money was not wanting, a faint
gleam of hope came in at last to brighten the great
efforts that were being made for his defence. His
family and connections were highly respectable
His father had been a sheriff of London, and, at the
imminent risk of his life, had prevented the rioters
of Lord George Gordon's day from bursting into the
large bullion-room of the Bank of England and
carrying off the gold. The sheriff thrust himself
before the gates and, with the greatest difficulty,
slipped the chain across the door, and eventually
stayed the progress of the mob. Apart from the
claims to consideration on his father's account, the
prisoner had, until the present discovery, proved
himself a most efficient servant of the Bank. But
at that time a spirit of gambling in the public
funds, only one degree less horrid than that of the
hells to which I had been accustomed, pervaded
many of the clerks of the Bank, and the prisoner
had become particularly infected by it, so much so,

that in one single speculation he lost a large sum
which he replaced by transferring the funds belonging to Sir Robert Peel to a feigned person named
William Penn, purposing, like most others who
abandon themselves to a similar delinquency, to
return them to the Bank when the expected stroke
of good fortune would place it in his power to
do so.

Notwithstanding his claims to merciful consideration, the Bank was resolved not to show the smallest
leniency, but, for the sake of a necessary example,
to prosecute the case to the utmost. But the result
proved what a lottery is law, or rather how much its
chances may be affected by the skilful intervention
of the god Plutus. The case was so clear against
the prisoner that the only object first aimed at was
to gain time by getting the trial postponed until
next sessions. My sympathies were of course
deeply stirred, and I should not be complying with
the dictates of truth, which, I trust the reader is
sensible, govern the whole of this history, if I did
not candidly acknowledge that I wished for the
acquittal of the prisoner. So far as my opportunities extended, I threw no obstacle in the way of
his obtaining it. As a matter of fact, he had re-

covered from the wounds and fractures received in his fall from the window, but I connived at his still remaining in bed, although when asked by the officer if he had sufficiently recovered to be able to stand his trial, I readily replied, " To be sure he is, as able as I am." Nothing further was accordingly said until the morning appointed for the trial, when he was ordered into Court, but the Judge and the Counsel for the Bank were not a little surprised when they saw him carried in on a litter and bandaged all round, as if still suffering from his half-healed fractures. The scheme succeeded, and the Court immediately ordered him back to give him time to recover by next sessions.

Time having been thus gained, no stone was left unturned, which money could by any possibility move, to get up a plausible defence. The solicitor for the Bank, in order to elucidate the alleged transfer of the stock to a person named William Penn, employed one of the most efficient Bow Street officers to ferret that individual out, if such a person actually existed. This of course, came to the knowledge of the prisoner's friends, who took care to throw, as if by accident, a little clue in the officer's way, by which he might trace the missing

man. The landlady of an inn, who had of course
received a consideration for her pains, solemnly
declared that a person answering the description of
Penn had suddenly left her house, where he had
been residing, when he heard of the arrest of the
prisoner. This formed the first of the links of a
chain which had been concerted to enable the Bow
Street officer to trace the fictitious Penn to a sea-
port town, where other persons were prepared to
prove that such a man had embarked at the time on
board a ship bound for America.

The two principal witnesses against the prisoner
were the subordinate clerks in the office in which he
was employed. When the first was called upon and
had sworn to the handwriting, the prisoner's
counsel, aware of the fact that he was an atheist,
which had not transpired before, cross-examined
him on the point with such success that his
evidence was rejected. The other witness also
failed the prosecution because he could not
remember seeing the prisoner s handwriting in the
transfer-book until after his apprehension, and such
was the influence of money on this occasion that
the very leaf on which the transfer had appeared
was not to be found when wanted, having been torn

out of the book. The consequence of all this was, that the witnesses for the Bank were completely baffled, everything was accounted for and cleared up to the satisfaction of the Court, and, after a ten hours' trial, the prisoner was acquitted on all the indictments.

CHAPTER VII.

PERSONS in the situation of the prisoner I have
just described are of course very differently affected
on entering Newgate as compared with the great
mass of criminals who pass through its sullen portals
every year. When the sensibilities of the heart are
drawn forth by the early culture of the mind, and
by the endearing excitements which social and
refined intercourse produces, the loss of character
entailed by a reverse of fortune or the ignominy of
a public condemnation, to say nothing of the stings
of conscience, is far more severely felt than it could
possibly be by one who had never tasted the
pleasures of society, whose education had been mainly
acquired in the schools of vice, and whose life had

been spent in the dissipations of idleness. It has often been said that the uncertainty of the law, and the mist that still envelops the fate of the criminal even when condemned, are great encouragements to delinquency. Even in capital offences the chances of escape are so many. But this, I conceive, is only half the evil effect of the uncertainty or gambling, as it may well be called, of the law. For by the same rule on which the criminal calculates the chances of escape, he frames his mind at the same time to the alternative of the last punishment. Common-sense tells us that this is only the simple process of cause and effect, operating on the material of human nature. Let the law be as lenient as you please, the more lenient perhaps the better, but let its punishments in all cases of conviction be certain and inevitable. As long as the world lasts or until the millennium begins, crime and all its train of misery will exist, but the light of reason and religion may doubtless do much to arrest its progress. The direct effect of the present system is to sear up and destroy the best faculties of human nature. Callousness and recklessness are its immediate consequences.

A criminal named M—, who among others had

been condemned to die, was placed under my charge
in the hospital, owing to some trifling complaint
with which he said he was afflicted. Had I been
so inclined, I might have had him sent out of the
hospital by showing how slight his illness was. But
under the painful circumstances, knowing that he
might be informed of the day of his doom at any
moment, I was unwilling to be harsh, and permitted
him to enjoy the comparative comforts that the
hospital afforded. He had fallen fast asleep one
evening when the Sheriff arrived to announce to
him the awful news that he was to be hanged next
Monday morning. The poor creature raised himself
in the bed, and, thinking I verily believe more of
the respect that was due to the Sheriff than of his
own dreadful situation, touched a little tuft of hair
that stuck out on his brow from underneath his
nightcap, and, bending his head, merely replied—
" Very well, gentlemen." Then lying down again
and drawing the blankets over his shoulder, he was
asleep and actually snoring in five minutes. Some
allege that a sincere repentance and a happy frame
of mind would under the circumstances bring about
such marked indifference to the near approach of an
ignominious death. My impression is that in this

particular case there was a total absence of all
feeling save that which arose, as with the insensible
brutes, from the simple cravings of nature.
Occasionally however I have seen the sway of a
ruling passion so strong as to be paramount even in
the last hour, and to swallow up every other feeling.
About the same time that the above incident
occurred, a greedy old man suffered the last penalty
of the law, and although his wife was in the most
destitute condition, and came frequently to the
prison begging him to afford her a small relief, he
would not give her a single sixpence. Knowing
full well he would die in a few days, he actually
went to the gallows and was hanged with nine
sovereigns in his trousers pocket while his wife was
in this starving condition.

Mr. Gibbon Wakefield, speaking of his prison
experiences, has declared that the prisoners, both in
and out of Newgate, are, almost without exception,
imbued with an ardent desire to be transported to
these colonies—a wish, he says, that induces many
to commit offences in order to realise this longing of
their hearts. The learned Archbishop of Dublin has
taken up the theme, and addressed two long letters
to Earl Grey, urging the impropriety, alike on moral

9

and political grounds, of continuing the present
system of transportation.   Now, upon the experience, not only of the twenty months I speak of,
but of the three years' imprisonment, which the
reader will presently see I subsequently endured, as
well as my nine years' close observance of convicts,
after their transportation to these colonies, I most
distinctly affirm that Mr. Gibbon Wakefield's con-
tention is not correct.

Let every man examine the emotions of his own
breast, and see whether in the abstract, and under
any circumstances, he would wish to be torn away
from those scenes of his youth which habit or
intimacy had endeared to his remembrance, from
old friends and relations to whom he felt he had a
natural right to look for sympathy and support in
periods of distress, and to be placed amidst a sunken
and degraded class, among strangers in a distant land!
Even the voluntary emigrant, with all his hope and
expectation of bettering his position in life, is not
without an inward pain, approaching, not unfrequently, to a species of torture, on so trying an
occasion.   How much more is the convict alive to
these acute sensations!   He is doomed to be landed
on a foreign shore, with the ensign of crime carried

before him, where his deprivation of liberty will consist, not, as in England, of simple confinement within prison walls, or of the exaction of labour, but in having the eye of supervision everlastingly over him, in being assigned to a master whose interest it is to watch him incessantly, and to deprive him of the smallest chance of indulging in his favourite propensities. No, the prisoners of Newgate fear nothing so much as transportation. From the moment that they enter the prison, the subject which most prominently occupies their minds is— how to evade this much-dreaded alternative. This is the fact, gainsay it who will, and let it be borne in mind that I speak from considerable experience, from personal knowledge of upwards of 15,000 individuals who came under my particular notice during my stay in Newgate.

The female prisoners were kept entirely by them selves in a separate part of the building. There were sometimes as many as 200, previous to the Sessions at the Old Bailey. A ladies' committee inspected the whole of the prison every Friday. I have seen from forty to fifty carriages collected at the gate on those occasions. The ladies gave out needlework to the female prisoners and paid them

9*

small sums. I remember a hearth-rug, upon which
four of them had worked, that was sold for ten
guineas. Mrs. Fry was a constant visitor. Amongst
other distinguished lady visitors, I once saw the
Princess of Denmark, who was then on a visit to the
English Royal family. The Countess of Darlington,
who accompanied Her Royal Highness, said to
me—" I wonder how you can keep this hospital so
neat and clean." "Please your ladyship," I replied,
" I have been used to a man-of-war." No employment was found for the male prisoners, as they were
drafted away to their respective destinations at the
close of each Sessions, with the exception of the
privileged few who, like myself, were permitted to
remain, and work about the prison in different ways
—cooks, sweepers, whitewashers, carpenters, wards-
men, etc. Every artifice is employed, and every
influence brought to bear by the prisoners to get
themselves appointed to these menial situations,
rather than be sent to the hulks, or transported.

My situation as hospital-assistant precluded me
from any desire or opportunity to yield again to my
ruinous failing. How great the importance of the
prayer, enjoined as one of the most essential by the
Divine Preserver and Teacher of mankind, to be

kept from temptation ! During this time, when I
had no temptation before me, my life was happy and
contented. Throughout the twenty months of my
sojourn in Newgate, I scarcely ever gave a thought
to gambling. Judging from my own experience in
this respect, I realised the efficacy of transportation
as a check to crime, for, when temptation is removed
from the convicts, all desire or inclination to offend
is removed at the same time. But even if I had
been viciously disposed, the unvarying kindness and
consideration of my immediate employer, Dr. Box,
would have effectually restrained me. None but
those who have filled subservient situations can
adequately share the feelings of him who has had
the satisfaction to serve a good master, or rightly
appreciate how much the good conduct of the
servant depends on that of the employer. That
person must be strangely constituted who would not
strive to give such a man as Dr. Box every satisfaction in his power, by his assiduity and uniformly
correct behaviour. And this enables me to illustrate
another feature of the assigned service transportation system. For, the settlers to whom the convicts
are for the most part assigned have a still stronger
and more personal motive to act the part of the

good master than Dr. Box ever had with me, seeing that their success as colonists mainly depends on the reformed conduct of their assigned servants. It is evident at a glance how different the influence of Dr. Box over me, or that of the settler over the assigned prisoner, is from that of the keeper or overseer of any gaol, penitentiary, or gang, where many men are subjected to the control of one who has only a collective interest in them.

Dr. Box was surgeon to other London prisons in addition to Newgate, and the responsibility of his position was very great. He once nobly and conscientiously withstood a bribe of a very large amount. It happened that a gentleman was confined for a capital offence, for which he had been tried and condemned to death. By his decease his family would lose the chief part of their patrimony, which consisted of a lease for life of certain Crown lands held at a low rate and yielding a handsome income. The two sons of the prisoner came to Dr. Box and offered him £4,000, with every assurance of secrecy, if he would certify that their father was insane, so as to avert the execution. Dr. Box rejected the bribe with indignation, but his sympathy for the distressed family induced him

to give a pledge not to divulge the circumstance
except to the Recorder, Sir John Silvester, who also
agreed to keep it secret. The sons subsequently
waited on two very eminent physicians in London,
and, by the offer of equally large bribes, succeeded
in getting a certificate of their father's insanity.
The case came before the Council, and Dr. Box was
summoned to attend. On entering, Lord Sidmouth
said :

"Take a chair, Mr. Box."

Whereupon Lord Eldon exclaimed :

"No, that man shall not sit down in my presence.
He has been guilty of a gross dereliction of duty in
not certifying that this person is mad, who has been
declared to be so by two physicians far more eminent
and skilful than himself."

The certificate of the two distinguished doctors
carried conviction to the minds of the Council; the
prisoner was liberated as being irresponsible for his
actions, and was soon amusing himself in his garden
and talking as rationally as ever. Sir John Silvester
afterwards informed Lord Sidmouth of the truth,
and eulogised the immovable firmness of Dr. Box in
resisting the bribe. The incident also came to the
ears of Lord Eldon, who sent for Dr. Box, apologised

for the apparent roughness of his first reception, and praised him as he deserved for his rigid adherence to personal and professional integrity.

During the intervals of duty in prison I devoted myself to reading and literary occupations. From the inexpensive manner in which I lived, and the various gratuities with which I was presented from time to time, I found my pockets tolerably well furnished on my liberation. The first person I met going along the street was my old friend, the captain of the whaling ship *Alexander*. Poor man! he had just emerged from the King's Bench prison, where he had been long confined for debt. I had scarcely parted with him when I had the pleasure to meet Captain King, whom I had known as Governor of New South Wales. He was then, he informed me, setting out for Bath to see his old friend, Captain Phillip, the first Australian Governor, who was lying dangerously ill. It was the last journey he ever took, for he died soon after his arrival, whereas Phillip recovered. His account of Norfolk Island is one of the most interesting works on the colonies.

I was never superstitious. Had I been so, I might have had a presentiment of my future fate

from the singular recurrence of former scenes and
incidents in Australia thus brought accidentally to
my remembrance. Little did I think then that I
was destined to endure so many years of bondage at
the Antipodes. Had it been made a condition of
my liberation that I should depart forthwith from
England, I should certainly have been saved from
my last dreadful lapse at the gaming-table, with its
lifelong ruinous consequences to me. But, as the
reader will remember, I was unfortunately permitted
to remain in England for a month, and with my
pockets tolerably well filled, I could not resist a
visit to my former wretched haunts. I was soon
once more within the grip of the gambling fiend,
and was gradually reduced to penury. I had also
overstayed my time in England by several weeks. I
was on the road to a tender in the river in order to
go on board a man-of-war, when I had the misfortune to meet an old acquaintance on Tower Hill,
whom I had known in Newgate. The scoundrel
invited me to dinner, and while we were enjoying
as I thought, friendly social conversation, he had
the police introduced into the house, and myself, his
guest, apprehended under his own roof. I was tried
and formally sentenced to death for violating the

condition of my liberation, but this was afterwards commuted to transportation for life. I had interest, however, to secure my re-appointment to my former situation in the hospital, where I remained for three years, but I never imagined for a moment that I should receive so severe a sentence for remaining a few weeks beyond my appointed time in England.

Immured once more within the walls of Newgate, I, for a time, mourned deeply over my hapless fate. Time, however, softened my regret, and I found some consolation in studious pursuits. I revised and retouched the published account of my three years' travels through France and Germany, subsequent to the battle of Waterloo. The object of that journey, which was to ascertain what effects the subjugation of the troops of Napoleon was likely to have in advancing the interests of British commerce, gave this book a character of importance which perhaps it would not otherwise have possessed. I also wrote the work which has since been published in England without my knowledge under the title of " The Religion of Christ the Religion of Nature," and which cost me no small amount of study and attention. Had it cost no more I should have been thankful. But the fact of my having written such

a work aroused hostility against me in certain
atheistical quarters, and a regular battery was
levelled against me, which did not cease its fire
until I was ordered on board the hulk *Justitia* to
be sent out with the first sailing transport ship to
these colonies. I was exceedingly surprised that
the Secretary of State should have listened to
the suggestions of these atheistical monsters and
ordered me for transportation, when, by the general
regulations, I was entitled to His Majesty's pardon.

CHAPTER VIII.

IN October, 1825, I was removed from Newgate to
the hulk *Justitia*, which was lying at Woolwich.
The moment a convict passes over the gangway of a
hulk, he is searched for money or other articles of
value ; he is then taken below, and entirely stripped,
is subjected to an ablution, has his hair cut off, and
a prison-dress put on ; irons are placed on his legs,
and next morning he is sent to hard labour in the
dockyard. A very few, as a matter of great favour,
are permitted to wear a slight bezel on one leg and
are exempted from dockyard labour. I was one of
those thus privileged. All communication with the
rest of the world is cut off, no person is allowed on
board, a visitor must stand on a platform by the
side of the hulk, and can only speak to a prisoner in

the presence of an officer. Any money or articles
given to a prisoner must be handed over to the
chief mate; all letters, even from members of
parliament, to a convict are opened, and if the
captain does not choose to deliver them, he need
not do so. In like manner, letters from convicts
to friends, relations and others are inspected, so,
should anyone complain, he only exposes himself to
vengeance and punishment. When a House of
Commons committee of inspection visits the hulks,
everything seems in admirable order, and when the
unfortunate men are asked if they have any
complaints to make, the reply is invariably in the
negative, for woe betide him who should dare to
open his lips except to say that the treatment on
board was most humane and kind. The superintendent of a hulk is styled captain and the
subordinate officers are called mates, although none
of them are seafaring men, being simply promoted
turnkeys. I have seen the captain knock a poor
fellow down with one blow merely for not getting
quickly out of his way when passing forward on the
deck. Redress is impossible, for all is mystery and
secrecy. I am bound to admit that I escaped any
harsh treatment, and it is only a sense of truth and

public utility that could impel me to state facts as they are.

I have long had by me several incidents of the hulks which I intended to have published, but a sense of shame prevented me from doing so and I now feel happy that the hulk establishments are broken up, for hitherto they have proved nothing but schools of abominable pollution. Those who have been discharged from them have overrun England and spread vice and immorality everywhere in their track. I scarcely ever saw any signs of true repentance in any of them ; on the contrary, most have, after their liberation, been again convicted, though by changing names they have succeeded in concealing the fact from the notice of the authorities. I am glad indeed that those establishments, those nuisances, those nurseries of deep crime, have been removed, for I should have felt reluctant to publish what I myself have seen in them. On board the hulks any one who should complain to the superiors concerning these heart-appalling scenes, would be destroyed by the other prisoners and would incur the resentment of the officers.

Should I be asked whether the whole, or at least

the greater portion, of the convicts on board the
hulks really merited the punishment inflicted upon
them, truth would compel me to answer in the
affirmative, but the whole system tended un-
equivocally to make them sycophants, hypocrites,
and ten times more the children of darkness than
they were before. Only those amongst them were
appointed to petty offices who would betray their
fellow-convicts, not in matters of great crimes or
attempts to escape, but in such little trivialities as
the unwarrantable possession of an inch of tobacco,
or a little tea and sugar, or half a loaf.

It was natural that, seeing myself surrounded
with horrors such as I have indicated, I should make
every interest to get away as speedily as possible
from scenes which afflicted me more than any I had
witnessed in the previous course of my life. I was
therefore delighted to receive the permission of the
Home Secretary to proceed to Van Diemen's Land
in the *Woodman*, which had been chartered to
convey convicts to that colony. I found the *Woodman* in all the hurry and confusion of preparing for
sea. The berths for the prisoners were not yet
finished; friends had come from all parts to take a
last farewell of those who were to be banished to a

distant land; swearing, cursing, wrangling, lamentations and tears offended all within hearing, and one would fancy ten thousand demons had been let loose. The Surgeon-Superintendent had not arrived, and consequently there was no check on the prisoners, the other officers having quite enough to do without heeding them. One would imagine that persons sent to a penal settlement in expiation of crimes committed at home would, when starting on their voyage across the seas, show some signs of contrition, and cease their former evil practices, but it was not so. By daylight or by dark they did not scruple to steal all that came in their way. Boxes and parcels of tea and sugar were torn from under those who possessed them, and one's life would be endangered by resistance to these ruffians. I remember one day when I had occasion to open a trunk in the single berth allotted to me, a silk handkerchief was snatched by someone, and on looking round to see who it was, I was served in a similar manner by others. Having taken most of the articles out of the box, many of them were thus stolen before I could replace them in security. Those who were most active and daring in these exploits were looked up to with a great deal of

respect by their less hardened fellow-convicts. It
may seem strange how such stolen articles could be
disposed of in a ship whose every hole and corner
was liable to inspection and search. But the
thieves easily found receivers, for wearing apparel
and many other articles were sold to the soldiers,
their wives, and the sailors in the half-deck.

The Surgeon-Superintendent now joined the ship.
He was of a meek and kind-hearted disposition, and
well qualified for his work, having already made two
voyages to the colonies with convicts and given
general satisfaction. Mr. Leary, a lieutenant in the
navy, commanded the *Woodman*, and Mr. Nutting,
the chief mate, was shrewd, honest and off-handed,
with much of the gentleman about him. Order
and regularity were soon established, and some of
the prisoners, whose characters stood fair, were
appointed to subordinate situations, such as
boatswain's mates, cooks, sweepers, etc. As I had
dabbled a little in medicine, I was placed in the
hospital as dispenser and assistant. Those who
were so selected enjoyed privileges to which the
other convicts were strangers, and were entitled to
go on deck nearly at all hours from sunrise to
sunset. I had forwarded a letter to my friends to

10

furnish me with some money, but our departure
was so sudden that the one addressed to me in
reply never reached me, although I have since been
charged with it in account.

The *Woodman* having received her final orders,
we sailed from Sheerness at the latter end of
November, with 150 convicts on board and a detach-
ment of military, the latter accompanied by their
wives and children in some instances. We had not
proceeded far down the Channel before we were
overtaken by a storm, and the ship laboured exceedingly. Little care had been evinced in examining the ship before she was chartered, for the
stem was so loose that an immense volume of water
poured into the hospital and made sad havoc with
all my arrangements. To those who had never been
at sea before the situation was intensely disagreeable, a large number of persons cooped up in small
berths, encumbered with irons, and dreadfully sea-
sick, combining to make up a scene of the most
repellent description. Yet comical incidents occur
in the most distressing circumstances. I remember
one night, when the sea was washing over the deck
and the water pouring down the hatchways. We
had a lamp burning in the hospital, and a stout

ignorant countryman came running in, praying that
we would lend him the lamp. I asked him what
did he want it for ? He exclaimed :

" We are all going down in this ship, and I
should like to see where I go to."

At length the weather abated, and we proceeded
along with a fair breeze. The hour arrived when
we gazed on the English shore for the last time. I
now found myself torn from all that was dear to me
on earth, from friends and relations whom I had not
seen for years, but with whom I had held friendly
intercourse. I stood in silent agony, taking a last
and lingering view of those shores the sight of
which had, on so many former occasions, afforded
me keen delight when returning to them after long
voyages to distant lands. I saw myself an exile
and a captive on that element on which I had once
been a commander. I felt the blow, and I felt it
deeply. I could scarcely quell the emotions which
swelled my unhappy breast without giving vent to
tears, but a sense of manhood restrained me from
any public exhibition of emotion. I then made a
fervent appeal to Heaven, and I have not prayed in
vain.

For the information of such as are not acquainted

10*

with the precise manner in which convicts are conveyed to the penal colonies, I will give a brief summary of the regulations. The British Government has hitherto regarded the transportation of prisoners as the chief mode of providing labour in the colonies. Punishment and utility have been connected so as to render convict labour alike beneficial to the colonists and conducive to the best interests of the parent state. All convicts sent out are newly clad, and ample rations of wholesome food are apportioned to them. Health is preserved by cleanliness, which is strictly attended to, and the ship-owners are bound by the terms of their charter to supply each prisoner with at least half-a-gallon of water per day. Care is also taken that they are not subjected to any oppressive or capricious treatment. Formerly, it frequently happened that brutal masters of convict ships would flog every prisoner on board. To prevent abuses of that sort, a surgeon of the Royal Navy has for some years past been attached to every convict-ship to superintend the prisoners on the passage out. This officer, in addition to his half-pay, is entitled to half-a-guinea per head for every prisoner he delivers safe and sound at the end of the voyage, on receiving

a certificate from the governor of the colony that his
conduct has merited such a gratuity. Naturally
under such a system surgeon-superintendents have
every inducement to exercise the greatest attention
and vigilance, and to see that everyone receives his
just allowance, which includes two pints of wine
served every week, as well as a certain quantity of
limejuice and sugar each day after arriving in the
warmer latitudes. Canisters of preserved meat are
supplied for the sick, with rice, tea, sugar, sago, and
extra wine, as well as an additional allowance of water.
Should a convict be deemed deserving of corporal
punishment, the superintendent and master must
both concur before it can be inflicted, and particular mention must be made in the ship's log-book
of the nature of the offence and the amount of
punishment awarded. During our passage from
England to the Cape of Good Hope, only two
convicts were flogged, and they richly deserved it,
having been caught in the act of robbing their
comrades.

After the Land's End had faded from our view,
all the prisoners were called on deck and relieved
of their irons. This relaxation threw an air of
cheerfulness over the ship, and with happier

countenances, we glided with gentle breezes over the swelling billows. As the prisoners conducted themselves extremely well, and were permitted to come on deck for a certain time every day, a general good-will prevailed on board, and the soldiers and sailors were alike very agreeable.

After crossing the tropic of Cancer, a number of the convicts were attacked by a species of brain fever, which speedily carried off four, who were buried in the deep. A considerable number had to be placed in the hospital. It certainly appeared to me that the surgeon was wrong in his treatment of the complaint. He sometimes gave in one dose from twenty to thirty grains of calomel, when the disease invariably terminated in madness. But, poor man! he was himself soon attacked with the fever, and one morning he suddenly dropped dead from his chair, to the grief of all on board. This sad event placed me in a position of great responsibility, for I was called upon to take sole charge of the hospital and do the best I could. By following the simple practice I had learned from Dr. Box in Newgate, I succeeded in restoring all the afflicted to their usual health, and when the *Woodman* arrived at the Cape, there was not a single individual in the hospital.

The master and officers were not permitted to
land by the Cape authorities, who supposed that
some epidemic disease was lurking in the ship.
But it was absolutely necessary according to the
regulations that we should be supplied with a
surgeon, and the Admiral on the station ordered
Captain Auckland, commanding a sloop of war, to
send his surgeon on board the *Woodman*. Mr.
Kelly was this gentleman's name, and he was
apparently glad to be removed to our ship. He was
uncommonly skilful in his profession, and possessed
great generosity. His history was rather singular.
He had served with distinction in the Navy, and at
the close of the war had settled down in a lucrative
practice at Belfast. He had married a young wife,
and it is well-known how a young wife can manage
a middle-aged husband. She was a Roman Catholic
and persuaded him on one occasion to attend an
anti-Orange demonstration. This was reported to
the Lords of the Admiralty, with the result that Mr.
Kelly was immediately ordered for active service.
A refusal to comply with this command would, of
course, have entailed the forfeiture of his half-pay.
What with being appointed to a sloop, removed from
a profitable practice, and compelled to leave his wife

behind, his temper had become somewhat soured,
and his brother officers did not always find him an
agreeable companion.

When the *Woodman* put out to sea once more,
it soon transpired that Mr. Kelly and the master,
though both Irishmen, were totally opposed to one
another in political principles.   The convicts
derived no small advantage from this conflict of
opinion, for if any one of them committed a breach
of discipline and the surgeon desired to have him
punished, the master would not consent, and *vice
versa.*   However, the prisoners continued to conduct themselves very quietly on the whole.   A
ludicrous incident occurred one evening when the
wind was blowing hard, and all hands were engaged
reefing and handing the sails.   Mr. Kelly turned
into his cot and was in the act of pulling a garment
over his head, but unfortunately he had forgotten
to remove a pair of strong silver sleeve-buttons,
and the ship at that moment taking a lurch,
he tumbled out and remained perfectly helpless
on the floor, rolling to and fro for some time,
the noise on deck being so great that no one
could hear his cries.   The accident was fortunately
attended with no more serious consequences than a

broken nose and a black eye. It is but bare justice
to Mr. Kelly to say that his undoubted skill, and
unremitting attention to the convicts, prevented any
disease from spreading amongst them, and only
one died between the Cape and Van Diemen's
Land.

On May 4, 1826, we arrived in the Storm Bay
passage and sailed up the river with a fair wind. I,
who had visited the scene twenty-four years
previously, when no white man occupied a single
spot in Van Diemen's Land, and when all around us
was a wilderness, felt myself strongly moved by the
changes that time and colonial energy had brought
about in my absence. Along the banks of the river
I observed a long series of farms and pleasant-
looking cottages, but it was when we reached the
harbour on the following morning that my astonishment became truly great. It has fallen to my lot
to visit many colonies and settlements on this globe,
and if I had not witnessed the amazing transform-
ation now disclosed to my view on the site where
Hobart Town reared its novel and beautiful aspect,
I could have formed no conception of it from any
published description, and I should have rejected
the truth as an exaggeration. In less than one

generation the foundations of future strength and prosperity had been laid.

My mind dwelt in deepest contemplation of the city that had sprung up during my wanderings in the northern hemisphere, and I brooded over the thought that twenty-four years ago I had assisted in forming the infant settlement on this very spot. Thinking of then and now, of the grievous change in the circumstances under which I revisited this scene of my former labours, I keenly felt the sad reverse of fortune, my head drooped, and I could scarcely refrain from weeping over my present helpless condition and my forlorn hopes. My imagination presented nothing but gloomy presages and a dreary waste during the remainder of my earthly pilgrimage. Mournful indeed were the prospects before me, yet I felt a cheering ray of hope that time would heal the deepest wounds, and that fresh energy and a constant reliance on Providence in this new and improving land would tend to blot out the harrowing memories of a dismal past, and conduce to a brighter future.

CHAPTER IX.

On the morning after the *Woodman* had anchored
in the harbour, the convicts were all landed in their
prison-clothes and marched in regular order to the
barracks, where they were drawn up in line and
inspected by His Excellency Colonel Arthur, the
then Governor of Van Diemen's Land. I had
brought with me letters of recommendation from
Mr. Pearse and Captain Dundas, both directors of the
Van Diemen's Land Company, to their principal
agent, Mr. Edward Curr. Unfortunately for me, I
did not avail myself of those testimonials, although
an application was made by Mr. Curr that I might
be assigned to the company's service. When the
Woodman was sailing up the river, she was boarded

by Mr. Rolla O'Farrell, a Government official of
fashionable appearance, who spoke a little French.
He accosted me, and, as I was informed that he was
of a humane disposition, I applied for permission to
be placed in his office rather than be assigned to
the Company. I soon discovered that I had committed a serious error, for the Government pay was
very small, a prisoner clerk receiving only sixpence
a day salary, and a shilling for rations, the former
paid every quarter and the latter every month. I
landed with a solitary one pound note in my
possession, and so was compelled to dispose of the
greater and best part of my wardrobe to obtain the
means of subsistence. Often when I saw prisoners
assigned to gentlemen, tradesmen and farmers,
sitting down to a plentiful repast, I felt inclined to
curse my unlucky stars that I was not brought up
as a labourer, servant, or handicraftsman of some
sort.

I certainly had hoped that the Governor would
have extended some consideration towards me in
view of my long incarceration in Newgate, and in
recognition of my services on board the *Woodman*
in having successfully supplied the place of the
surgeon for five weeks. But I was disappointed.

Under the *regime* of Colonel Arthur, prison discipline had assumed a very different and much more
stringent character than before. In former days
pardons were easily obtained, not so now. Besides,
strange rumours were afloat which tended to make
the Governor somewhat circumspect in his dealings
with me. Some said I had been punished for
having written pamphlets against the British
Government and for having been a spy in England.
Others reversed this story and declared that the
British Government had employed me as a spy in
foreign countries, and Heaven knows what else
equally ridiculous and void of truth. The effect
of such stupid irresponsible stories was to create a
prejudice against me in official quarters. I was
told by Mr. O'Farrell that when an application was
made to Colonel Arthur on my behalf, the Governor
replied :

" I can do nothing for Jorgenson, as he is a
violent political character, and a dangerous man in
any country."

In this dilemma I made renewed and persistent
efforts to be transferred from the service of the
Government to that of the Van Diemen's Land
Company. I met with many difficulties, for the

removal of a clerk from a public office in the colony
was not readily sanctioned. However, my services
to the authorities were comparatively useless, for,
although I could write a tolerably fair hand, I was
quite incompetent to manage books of accounts and
entries. After a good deal of teasing, I was at
length assigned to the Company's service, and had
no longer any fear of want.

After some preliminary training in the office, I
was sent into the interior with a party of men to
explore the Company's land, and trace a road from
the River Shannon to Circular Head. We set out
early in September. During the whole of the winter
it had rained almost incessantly, and the rivers were
exceedingly swollen. We had to carry our provisions and necessaries in knapsacks on our backs, and
this not only impeded our movements but severely
taxed our strength, for each man was burdened with
six weeks' provisions. I had now arrived at a time
of life when such a task as this was not easy of performance, nevertheless I proceeded along cheerfully,
for roaming at large was much more agreeable to
my temperament than being cooped up in an office.
We visited a number of farms on our way, and
everywhere met with a most hospitable reception.

At that time some parts of the country were
infested with bushrangers, and the aborigines were
also becoming troublesome. More than eight days
elapsed before we could find a practicable ford across
the Shannon, and even then the water was up to
our arm-pits. Owing to the heavy knapsack I was
carrying and the fact that the stream was running
at the rate of six or seven miles an hour, I lost my
equilibrium, and would most assuredly have been
drowned if a member of my party, Black George,
had not providentially seized and saved me. At
length we all got across in safety, and proceeding
onwards in a north-westerly direction we arrived at
the Big Lake, a magnificent sheet of water. From
the heights around we enjoyed an extensive and
picturesque view of the charming lake country. On
approaching the River Ouse we again found ourselves in a dilemma, as no fording-place could be
discovered. We followed the river upwards for
many miles until we came upon a cataract environed
by perpendicular and seemingly impracticable rocks.
Just as we were about giving up the idea of further
progress as hopeless, a kangaroo bounded past us,
our dogs pursued the animal, and to our surprise we
were led through an opening which brought us

round to the north-west side of the rocks. We
eventually found a fording-place and crossed, though
not without imminent danger, for the water was high
and the stream rapid. After proceeding some distance
further on our tour of exploration, surrounded by
swollen rivers, deep gullies, and snow-covered mountains, our provisions began to show unmistakable
signs of exhaustion, and I determined to fall back
upon the Shannon for fresh supplies. We succeeded
in reaching the farm and cottage of Dr. Ross,
situated at the confluence of the Ouse and the
Shannon. On our arrival we learned that the
place had been visited on the previous day by a
daring and notorious bushranger named Dunn, who
had terrorised the inmates, insisted on the best
entertainment being provided for him, and eventually walked away, after having helped himself to
supplies of ammunition and provisions. How one
outlawed ruffian could carry everything before him
in this unquestioned style seemed somewhat
mysterious to me, until I remembered that a considerable number of the assigned servants all over
the country were actually in league and sympathy
with the bushrangers.

Having despatched one of my men to Hobart

Town with letters for Mr. Curr, the manager of the Company, I explored the country around in every direction. I generally went by myself, armed with a ponderous sword, presented to me by Dr. Ross. I have often wondered that I did not meet with bushrangers or some of the aborigines during these lonely wanderings. In my rambles I frequently met a Caledonian named Scott, who had come a free man to the colony, and had engaged as a shepherd in the service of a gentleman who possessed a fine sheep-run in that part of the country. Scott was an inoffensive, well-behaved man, who by frugality and sobriety had succeeded in saving £400. I frequently conversed with him and learnt that some of the aboriginal tribes were in the habit of visiting his hut or meeting him on the run. For years he had been on the best of terms with them. He described them as a harmless race if not wantonly provoked or injured. He never carried firearms or any other weapons for his protection, and he smiled at the idea of his ever being assailed by the blacks.

Two days after I had been speaking with Scott as usual, a large tribe of blacks came down to a hut occupied by three assigned convict servants. These

11

men struck a bargain with some of the blacks and
afterwards succeeded in cheating them, which so
exasperated the blacks, nearly one hundred in
number, that they surrounded the hut and would
have certainly burnt it to the ground and killed its
inmates, had not the bushranger Dunn with some
members of his gang appeared on the scene and
compelled them to beat a retreat. In their rage
and disappointment at not getting their revenge,
the blacks fell in with poor Scott; the friendship of
former days was now entirely forgotten, and they
murdered him in a most barbarous manner.

This bushranger, Dunn, had a long-standing
grudge against a Mr. Thomson, a magistrate
residing near New Norfolk. The bold robber had
just previously made a descent upon Mr. Thomson's
farm, loosened a large, fierce dog from the chain,
and taken the animal away with him. It may seem
incredible that a stranger could quietly remove a
ferocious watch-dog, but the process is easily
effected. The bushranger places a large piece of
mutton, beef, or kangaroo on the fire and half broils
it. Then he takes it to windward of the dog, which
soon smells the appetising morsel and evinces an
impatience to get at it. When it is thrown within

reach, the animal eagerly devours it, and suffers itself to be led away. After having thus secured Mr. Thomson's dog, Dunn took it away with him for some distance, and, having killed a sheep, threw a quarter to the dog, exclaiming to one of Mr. Thomson's servants, whom he had compelled to accompany him :

" Now go and tell your master that I stole his dog at New Norfolk, and fed it with his own mutton here."

The history of one bushranger is the history of all such lawless desperadoes—sometimes suffering incredible hardships, anon revelling in plenty, and from mere wantonness or revenge needlessly destroying what they cannot carry away; betrayed by their own associates or by persons in whom they are necessarily obliged to place confidence, and finally expiating their crimes on the scaffold. Similarly, it may be said that the description of the mode in which one tribe of aborigines organised and carried out an attack on the whites would answer equally well for all. In every case there is the same resort to cunning and artifice, the same untiring patience in lying in wait for their prey, and the same barbarous cruelty with which their

11*

victims are murdered when once within their grasp. Their ceaseless vigilance to guard against surprise, and the dexterity they evince in eluding the closest pursuit are also noteworthy characteristics of theirs.

On the return of my messenger from Hobart Town, we resumed our interrupted tour of exploration, and succeeded in penetrating to the source of the Derwent. I was in hopes of reaching Circular Head, some 65 miles distant, when our progress was suddenly arrested by an impracticable country and impassable chasms. Our provisions were at a low ebb, and a hundred miles separated us from the nearest stock-hut in the settlements from which we had travelled. I calmed the apprehensions and the evident impatience of my men by assuring them of my ability to lead them to some stock-hut. Descending from the mountains and keeping between the flooded rivers, we gradually, to my great relief, entered on a grassy country sloping to the southward, and came upon broad cattle-tracks that told us plainly we were approaching the borders of civilization. Soon we caught sight of the Table Mountain on the Clyde, and our spirits were raised by the presence of that familiar landmark. By this time all our provisions were gone, nevertheless, we

started cheerfully at daybreak next morning, knowing that we could not be more than 30 miles from
the stock-hut, which to our inexpressible satisfaction
we reached at about three o'clock in the afternoon.
As we approached, the occupants of the hut regarded
us with general suspicion and some symptoms of
fear.   Our clothes were in tatters, our beards of
patriarchal length.   As we were carying fire-arms
and other weapons, we were evidently mistaken
for bushrangers.   I found some difficulty in con-
vincing the inmates of the hut that we were a party
in the service of the Van Diemen's Land Company,
but when we all laid down our arms, and when I
exhibited my map, compass, journals and letters
from Mr. Curr, their doubts were dispelled and they
treated us with the greatest hospitality and kindness.   At a farmhouse which we subsequently struck,
our appearance so frightened the inmates that they
barricaded themselves within the building and
could not be induced to open the doors on any
account.   They had good reason for their distrust,
for the house had been already thrice robbed by
bushrangers, and the family very harshly treated.
Luckily a shipmate of mine, coming from the fields
to his dinner, recognised me and mutually satis-

factory explanations ensued.   Without any further
adventures worth noting we arrived at Hobart Town,
where I delivered the report of my journey to the
authorities of the company.

From what I then learned I found we had good
reason to congratulate ourselves cn not having
continued our journey to Circular Head.   It had
been arranged that some casks of provisions and
clothing should be deposited there in anticipation
of our arrival, but a number of untoward circumstances prevented these supplies reaching their
destination, and we would have been exposed to all
the horrors of starvation if we had not altered our
programme.

After some more exploration journeys through the
bush, which I have described in detail in my
published account of "The Rise, Progress and
History of the Van Diemen's Land Company," I
was directed in the early part of January, 1827, to
proceed to Launceston, there to join the *Tranmere*,
one of the company's vessels, which was about to
convey to Circular Head hired servants, stores,
provisions, etc., for the purposes of an infant settlement.   A mutiny had broken out amongst the
convicts who were first sent to the place, and some

coercion was required to put it down, but coercion is at all times unpleasant, and often not attended with the desired effect. So Mr. Curr requested me, on my arrival at Circular Head, to exercise my influence over the prisoners and show them the injury they were doing themselves by not remaining quiet and obedient. This commission I easily accomplished, for in truth the prisoners had nothing serious to complain about ; their working hours were from six in the morning until six at night, they had proper time for meals, and they received ample rations and good warm clothing and bedding.

Soon after my arrival at Circular Head, I was placed in charge of a party under instructions to proceed along the western coast of Van Diemen's Land, and endeavour to penetrate as far as the Shannon. A whale-boat with provisions accompanied us for the first five days of our journey. We then loaded our knapsacks with supplies and ammunition, and accompanied by three kangaroo dogs, started on our march through this unexplored part of the island. As a precautionary measure, we buried 32lbs. of flour in two strong bags and made a large fire over the spot, so that the natives might not perceive that the ground had been dug. Mr.

Lorymer, one of the company's surveyors, was
with us, and we formed a little party of four. We
were not prepossessed with the country through
which we passed at first. The view towards the
coast was wild and forbidding, and, when we
ascended Mount Norfolk and other lofty eminences,
the scenery on every side was stern and savage.
In many places, as far as the eye could reach, the
view resembled the undulations of the ocean when
ruffled by a furious storm. On some parts of
the coast we fell in with the wrecks of vessels
buried in the sand, which had been piled up in
some places to an amazing height. At one
spot in particular a mountain of sand had been
reared, which we ascended with great difficulty and
found to be fully seven miles in length. The
farther we advanced the greater became our
difficulties. When we reached the Pieman's River,
it took us a whole day to descend from the top of
the bank to the water's edge, for the descent was
so precipitous that a false step would have cast us
headlong to destruction. The ascent on the
opposite bank was still more trying, and it took
us nearly two days to accomplish it. It was for the
most part sheer climbing up the perpendicular.

At the few spots where it was possible to pause and
rest awhile, we looked out upon a truly appalling
scene. All was desolation and chaos, as if some
mighty convulsion had rent the earth asunder and
sported with trees of enormous height and circumference, tearing them up by the roots and strewing
them around in reckless confusion. At length we
gained the heights and recognized in the distance
the Frenchman's Cap and the Traveller's Guide, two
well-known landmarks in the vicinity of Macquarie
Harbour. From the elevation we had now attained
I saw with considerable satisfaction what I supposed
to be extensive grassy plains stretching away to the
westward. We all thought we had discovered good
country and had gained the object of our expedition,
so we cheerfully descended. But when we approached the supposed luxuriant plains, what was
our disgust and disappointment to find ourselves
amongst six-wire scrub, so high, that when we
entered it, we could see none of the surrounding
objects. We cleared a way with our hackers, but
with all our efforts could not progress more than
200 yards in a day. The horrible truth then
flashed upon me that we were in that impenetrable
region where so many previous exploring parties

and runaway convicts from Macquarie Harbour
had been lost. We determined to retreat in all
haste to Circular Head, for our provisions were
shrinking fast and our two best dogs had died of
hunger. Not a solitary kangaroo was to be seen
in this sterile and inhospitable region. Our last
supplies were exhausted when we reached the spot
where we had made an underground deposit in
case of emergency, and to my inexpressible relief
we found the two bags of flour untouched and
intact. With our knapsacks thus replenished we
resumed our retreat, meeting from time to time
with huts constructed by the aborigines on quite
a different principle to that which prevails in other
parts of the island. They were very neatly built
and well thatched, shaped like a beehive, and
would easily accommodate about thirty persons.
The natives reside in these huts at certain seasons
of the year. We frequently traced their footprints
in the sands and on the sea-shore, but we could
never succeed in bringing them to a stand.

At Cape Cameron dangers began to thicken
around us once more, and for two days we could
find no drinkable water. We endeavoured to cross
the flats on the sea-shore, but the attempt was a

failure, for we sank knee-deep and, in our exhausted condition, it was only with the utmost
difficulty we could extricate ourselves. Finding no
means of fording the Duck River, we constructed a
raft of such dead timber as we could collect. I was
the first to venture upon it; and I had scarcely
done so when it went down, end foremost, and I
narrowly escaped being drowned. Proceeding
further up the river, we were still unsuccessful in
discovering a way of getting across. Next morning
Mr. Lorymer proposed that we should retrace our
steps and, somehow, endeavour to cross at the
mouth of the river. He said he could swim a little,
and as the spits of sand and mud ran out a considerable distance, he did not anticipate any
danger. But to make sure, we cut our blankets in
strips and made a sort of rope, which we fastened
around him. Poor Lorymer then led the way; all
at once we saw him plunge; the men behind
unfortunately pulled hard on the blanket rope; it
broke; our unfortunate companion made a second
plunge, and we lost sight of him for ever. This was
one of the saddest incidents of my life, and it made
an indelible impression on my mind. The sight of
my comrade, in the full vigour of life and health,

coming to so untimely an end, affected me very
deeply. I upbraided myself for having yielded to
his desire of returning to the mouth of the river,
and I regretted my acquiescence all the more when
we retraced our course up the river, for we had not
proceeded far above the place where we had camped
on the previous night, when we came upon a fallen
tree stretched right across the stream and forming
a bridge, over which we passed with ease. But we
were so exhausted that we could move no farther,
and we remained on the river-bank for the night.
The slightest weight was now most irksome to our
enfeebled frames, and we left our fire-arms and
everything else we could dispense with behind us
in the scrub. Next morning, although we knew we
could not be very far from our destination, we could
scarcely move our limbs, and I believe we would
never have returned alive to Circular Head, but for
our good fortune in coming upon a dog-fish, at
which the crows and the gulls were greedily
pecking. We seized upon this prize, and in a
moment it was cooked in a small camp-kettle, with
plenty of salt and pepper, the only articles that
remained in our knapsacks. Somewhat revived by
this lucky meal, we proceeded on our way, and

reached Circular Head in the afternoon, having tasted no food for four days, with the exception of the providential fish we had snatched from the ravenous crows and gulls.

CHAPTER X.

I GRADUALLY recovered from the exhaustion that supervened on this perilous and ill-fated expedition, and found that, during our absence, the advances and improvements which had been made at Circular Head were quite surprising. It had become a really bustling little place, yet good order, regularity, and steady management were everywhere apparent. A notable instance of the jealousy with which the blacks regard the loss of one of their women came under my notice here. A black girl from Cape Grim had attached herself to one of the white men at Circular Head, and no persuasion could induce her to rejoin her tribe. But they watched her incessantly; and one day, when she was a short

distance outside the settlement, she was suddenly
attacked by her own people, and received three or
four spear-wounds. She succeeded in escaping to
the settlement, and our surgeon cured her injuries;
but she ever afterwards lived in constant apprehension of attack.

In May 1827 I was informed that the Government had been pleased to grant me a ticket-of-leave,
which entitles a prisoner of the Crown, under certain
restrictions, to do the best he can for himself and
seek such employment as he deems most suitable
and beneficial. But should he misconduct himself
in any way, or be discovered out after a certain hour
in the evening, or miss the weekly muster, a single
magistrate may deprive him of the indulgence and
return him to the Government, when his case
becomes far worse than before, as a black mark is
entered against his name for not making a proper
use of the favour that had been extended to him.

I was now invited to assist in editing a newspaper
at Hobart Town, and I accepted the appointment,
as I was glad to employ myself in any way in which
I could earn an honest subsistence. But the worthy
proprietor insisted on every one in the house
attending prayers three times a day, and as these

prayers were unusually long, and delivered in a tone
and dialect that were extremely disagreeable, I
was soon very glad to terminate the connection.
Applying to the Government for employment, I
had the satisfaction of being nominated as a
constable of the field police, and assistant-clerk to
Mr. Thomas Anstey, the police-magistrate of the
Oatlands District. I had now to enter upon
duties to which hitherto I had been quite un-
accustomed. My district was more than 150 miles
in circumference, and as the habitations were
widely scattered, bushrangers were harassing the
settlers, and the hostile aboriginal tribes were
committing many murders and depredations, my
situation was not without its dangers and
difficulties. I had to visit all the farms and stock-
huts in the districts of Oatlands, Clyde, Campbell
Town, the Great and Little Swan Ports, and not
unfrequently Richmond. Some settlers, I found,
kept their convict servants under the strictest
discipline, whilst others neglected even the slightest
surveillance. It frequently happened that when I
made inquiry of some of my former shipmates and
acquaintances as to the character of certain individuals, I would be told :

" Oh, he is a fine man ; he will do what is right."

Of others it would be said:

" He is a rogue in grain and would be glad of a chance to injure any one."

The magistrate often felt extremely surprised at this, for the parties who would be lauded in this fashion had long been suspected of cattle and sheep-stealing and other malpractices, and those whose characters had been apparently depreciated were esteemed as honest and industrious men. But I was not slow in discovering the proper meaning and value of the information thus received. What was meant by calling a man a fine fellow and saying he would do what was right, was that he would join in any species of robbery and under no circumstances, not even from the gallows, divulge anything that might bring a companion to justice. By a rogue in grain was implied any one who would not join in robberies and plunders, and who would exert his utmost power to detect and punish villany.

The Government of Van Diemen's Land had ever found it a matter of extreme difficulty to establish a police that would devote their whole attention to the protection of life and property. Even the

12

highest pay that could possibly be given would not
induce free persons to encounter ferocious and
desperate bushrangers, pursuing them across
dangerous rivers into their mountain fastnesses, and
following in their tracks by day and night. Still
more severe was the service against the hostile
aborigines, for, with them, exertions almost beyond
human endurance could effect but little. The
prospect of freedom was the only stimulus that
could rouse convicts to risk their lives in defence
of the settlers and their families. Mr. Anstey was
pleased to say that I was an intelligent man and to
repose his confidence in me, giving me liberty to
exercise a large discretion in the discharge of my
duties. As regards sheep and cattle stealers, and
robbers of all sorts, persons illegally selling spirits
without a license, and all offenders of that stamp, I
followed them up with unswerving perseverance.
The sly grog-shops, particularly in the interior,
were nests for convicts of every description, robbers
were harboured in them, and stolen goods were
stored within their walls. As to such minor
offences as drunkenness, slight quarrels, and being
out a little beyond the prescribed hours, I did not
pay much heed to them, knowing that when police

are looking after such paltry matters the greater villains escape.

Notwithstanding the severity of the service, and the frequent necessity of travelling by myself over an extensive and lawless district, I found this mode of life so suitable to my temperament that I was scarcely ever more happy than at this time. For some years I enjoyed an unwonted tranquillity and serenity of mind. I received nothing but kindness from . Mr. Anstey, his lady and family, and all beneath his hospitable roof. I look back upon this period as one of the brightest in my life. I was free from care, and all anxiety was banished from my mind.

Whilst holding office as Constable at Oatlands, I devoted myself to an object which the governor, Colonel Sir George Arthur, and the magistracy had very much at heart. When Sir George first arrived in the colony, such was the state of society that he found it necessary to act with greater severity towards offenders than was consonant with his feelings. But sheep and cattle-stealing, highway robberies, and bushranging, often attended with murder, continued to disturb the public peace and place in jeopardy the lives and property of the

12*

colonists. The punishment of death was resorted
to, but with very little remedial effect. At the
period of which I am now speaking, a formidable
gang of sixty desperadoes acted in concert, and,
being connected with certain receivers in Hobart
Town and Launceston, were easily enabled to
dispose of their ill-gotten booty. If any person
accidentally passed whilst these scoundrels were
engaged in killing or driving away stolen stock, he
was immediately put to death. I remember one
unlucky trespasser who was seized, wrapped up in a
green bullock-hide, and roasted alive before an
immense fire. After a time, information was
obtained that led to the apprehension of the
principal depredators, but, instead of condemning
them all to death as hitherto, several were admitted
as evidence for the Crown. This new departure was
entirely successful, for almost the whole of the gang
were soon secured. Formerly a convicted prisoner
was induced from a false sense of honour to mount
the scaffold and die with his secrets, a decision due
also to the certainty that, no matter what he might
divulge, his life would not be spared. But when
the outlaws found that there were hopes of escaping,
they betrayed each other as fast as they could, and

the moral effect on the fraternity still at large was
of the most efficacious description, for all confidence
was destroyed, and no one knew whom he could
safely trust. The satisfactory consequence was,
that for two or three years afterwards sheep and
cattle-stealing were almost unknown crimes. Owing
to my activity in bringing about this improved
state of things, I incurred the enmity of the robbers
and their sympathisers, and I cannot but congratulate myself on my singular good fortune in
escaping the effects of their animosity. I am afraid
some innocent persons lost their lives through
being mistaken for me. Several murders were
committed in places to which I had frequently
resorted, and in huts where I had slept by myself
with no other protection than my trusty sword.

When I first set out on these journeys, I was
very much surprised at the sanguinary and repulsive
names given to many places I came across. Amongst
them were " Murderer's Plains," " Murderer's Tier,"
" Deadman's Point," " Killman's Point," " Hell's
Corner," " Hell's Gates," " Four-square Gallows,"
" Devil's Backbone," etc. Foreigners reading a
catalogue of such terrific titles would be apt to
think us a savage and peculiar people. It was also

the fashion to name places after some of the most notorious bushrangers, as if those depredators had performed actions worthy of commemoration.

In the early part of 1829 Sir George Arthur was roused to action by the alarming depredations of the aboriginal tribes of the island, who were carrying on a species of warfare against which the whites were unable effectually to contend. Such was the cunning displayed by the blacks in their attacks that all our measures were baffled, and many colonists were barbarously murdered. I was engaged for some time with a party of men under my orders in restraining the outrages of the blacks. I am aware it is said by some that bushranging and our broils with the blacks are traceable to the injudicious measures of Sir George Arthur, and that he was responsible for jeopardising the lives of the colonists and their property in the interior. People have boasted that if their advice had been taken, the blacks would have been captured at once and much blood would have been spared. They counselled the governor to send out a number of prisoners to catch all the aborigines and transport them to some island off the coast, but in what manner this desirable end could be achieved they did not say.

The fact is, that long before the arrival of Sir George Arthur, the blacks had engaged in systematic attacks on the whites. I could quote numerous instances, but shall only mention the case of Mr. Robert Jones, a respectable settler in the district of the Upper Clyde. His experience was unfortunately typical of many other settlers. He was residing in a stock hut, under a stony sugar-loaf, about two miles to the west of the Macquarie River. He had three companions, one of whom ran into the hut one afternoon in an exhausted condition, with the report that the natives were spearing the sheep and had pursued him until he came within sight of the hut. Mr. Jones and his companions seized their fire-arms and, after advancing 200 yards, descried the natives, who ran up into a high tier, where they were joined by a considerable number of their tribe. Some of the most daring of them now approached the whites, quivering their spears and making a hideous noise. Mr. Jones and his party presented their pieces, but soon discovered to their dismay that the man who had charge of the ammunition had unfortunately lost it. There was nothing for it but to beat a retreat, and the hut was reached in safety. Next morning the blacks came towards the hut in formidable array.

some carrying lighted bark in their hands, whilst
others took up a position on the side of the hill,
from which, after having given a loud shout, they
commenced to throw spears, waddies and stones at
the hut and its inmates.   They were smeared all
over with red ochre, a certain indication that they
were on the war-path.   Altogether they numbered
not less than 200 and were under the command of
a gigantic chief, who stood aloof from the rest,
issued his orders with the utmost calmness and
was implicitly obeyed.   Under his direction they
arranged themselves in crescent formation and made
a determined assault upon the hut, but were repulsed
and compelled to retreat.   A second furious rush of
the whole body was more successful, the whites had
to evacuate the hut and flee for their lives, pursued
by the howling horde.   Mr. Jones was struck by three
spears, one through the right cheek, another through
the right arm, and a third in the side.   A fortunate
accident saved the fugitives from massacre.   A
chance shot from one of their guns hit the aforesaid
gigantic chief and killed him on the spot.   The
blacks surrounded their fallen chief, tried to make
him stand erect again, and, seeing that their efforts
were unavailing, raised an unearthly yell, sent a

shower of spears to the skies, and violently smote
their breasts. In the confusion caused by this
accident Mr. Jones and his companions succeeded
in effecting their escape. On another occasion Mr.
Jones and his family were besieged for four hours
by a party of blacks, whom he somewhat paradoxically
describes as "swearing at us in good English."
This time their lives were saved by a courageous
and faithful little girl, a member of their household,
who crawled out unperceived and brought up a party
to their relief. After such critical experiences as
these, it is not surprising that Mr. Jones and his
men should ever afterwards place their fire-arms
against a stump in the middle of the field when
they went out ploughing.

It cannot be denied that ignorant and vindictive
stock-keepers often wantonly fired at and killed the
blacks, but it is no less true that the natives were
often guilty of gross ingratitude towards those who
had treated them with kindness. I remember a
party of blacks camping for three or four weeks at
a short distance from Mr. Anstey's, and, although
they were supplied every day with provisions from
the house, this kindness did not prevent them
from subsequently attacking two of Mr. Anstey's

men and robbing them of everything they possessed.

As the aborigines persisted in their depredations with the utmost daring—121 outrages were committed in the neighbourhood of Oatlands alone, and Mr. Anstey, as coroner, had to hold 28 inquests on the bodies of men, women, and children, victims of the blacks—it was only natural that the Governor should feel extremely uneasy and alarmed at the numerous reports of outrages which he daily received. He instituted a system of roving parties to go in pursuit of the blacks, and the direction of four of these bodies was assigned to me. It was a very laborious task, for I had sometimes to lead out one, and sometimes another, in the middle of winter, besides having to regulate the movements of all. The necessities of the case demanded that I should carry a heavy knapsack on my back, containing a whole month's provisions. When the roving parties were fully organised and equipped, Sir George Arthur issued instructions that would at once tend to the protection of the colonists and of inoffensive blacks. With that object certain boundaries were fixed beyond which martial law could not operate, and it was thought that when the blacks would find

by experience that there were certain parts of the
island in which they were never molested, they
would remain in those districts in peace and quiet-
ness.

The parties under my direction met with only
partial success so far as capture was concerned, but
there can be but little doubt that many lives were
saved by the activity and vigilance of the roving
bands which would otherwise have been sacrificed,
for the blacks could not with any safety approach
the stock-huts as hitherto, nor could they hunt or
light their fires within the settled districts without
being speedily driven back over the boundary lines.
But we laboured under great difficulties owing to
our ignorance of the numerical strength of the
aborigines. Reports of depredations crowded in
upon us from many different points and opposite
directions, and we came to the conclusion that the
blacks had a regularly organised system for distract-
ing our attention. One afternoon we surprised a
tribe under the western tier, encamped on the bank
of a small rivulet. Although we came suddenly
upon them, the slight noise we made in crossing the
rivulet alarmed them, and in an instant they dis-
appeared like so many spectres, without the possi-

bility of tracing them, leaving their spears, waddies, and plunder behind. The latter consisted of blankets, tea, sugar, firearms, cooking utensils and many other articles, which we identified as having been taken from places at considerable distances apart, clearly showing that the same tribe was continually moving on all points.

I was altogether two years in quest of the blacks, and during the whole of that period not a single complaint was made either against me or any of my parties, neither had I occasion to make any.

CHAPTER XI.

A VERY gratifying incident occurred at this time
which, as it placed me in a condition of comparative
freedom, forms a very important epoch of my life.
I happened to be at Anstey Barton one Saturday
when the mail arrived, and in looking over the
Gazette I observed my name announced as having
obtained a conditional pardon. I felt extremely
surprised, not having made any application for such
a boon. The kind inmates of Anstey Barton seemed
to derive even more satisfaction from the happy
event than I did myself. The fact is, a man who
has long been deprived of liberty may be compared
to one who has been bed-ridden for a considerable
time, and who, when allowed to walk, does not at

once feel his legs under him. So it was with me.
It was some time before I could shake off the
trammels in which I had hitherto been entangled.
Those who have always enjoyed freedom can form
only an inadequate idea of the feelings of one who
has just recovered his liberty after a protracted
period of bondage. Take the chain off the dog ; he
indulges in a variety of pranks, and all his former
ferocity deserts him.

I have more than once referred to the present
system of prison discipline, and to the employment
of convicts in the police force and wherever the
public safety required activity, diligence, patient
endurance, courage, and even daring. In this connection I will mention a curious and significant
incident. Prior to my receiving a pardon, I had
fearlessly plunged into rushing torrents with a
knapsack on my back weighing from 60 to 70lbs
On resuming my quest of the blacks, I proceeded to
Mr. George Espie's farm on the Jordan. Across the
Jordan at this point there runs a post-and-rail fence,
along which persons may pass over, although the
operation is not without danger, the fence trembling
from the heavy pressure of the current. I went
down and, although I had frequently crossed when

the fence was completely under water, and now there was a clear rail, yet I could not bring myself to venture the passage. Mr. Espie expressed his surprise at my backwardness, as he had formerly seen me cross without any apprehension.

"Yes, Mr. Espie," I replied, "but you forget that I was a prisoner then, and life was a matter of little moment, but now I am free, and I must take more care of myself."

Here, then, is the secret why convicts have exerted themselves and so often risked their lives for the public good and the general safety.

Notwithstanding our increased exertions and activity, the blacks became more cunning and experienced every day. Until now they had scrupulously refrained from travelling by night, as they entertained some superstitious notions on this head. Instead of remaining as before on the plains and by the side of the rivers, they now formed retreats in the high and rugged mountains, from which they could sally forth when the coast seemed clear. We had no suspicion that they could exist in places so inhospitable and so difficult of access, and it was some time before I discovered how matters really stood. Meanwhile, they were becoming more desperate every day. From their concealed positions on the heights, they closely watched the movements of the roving bands, and when one of these retired from a farm-house, they would immediately make a hostile descent in force. In one instance they noiselessly advanced on a farm-house our party had just visited, entered by the back door, killed the lady of the house and the children, and succeeded in getting away with a considerable amount of plunder. This daring outrage was perpetrated while the master and servants were at work in the field, not 50 yards from the front of the house, with firearms ready to their hands.

The unabated outrages of the blacks at length determined Sir George Arthur to make a call on the public spirit of the colonists. By proclamation His Excellency called out a levy *en masse* to cope with the crying evil of the day. It was vain to expect, he pointed out, that the country could be freed from the incursions of the savage tribes unless the settlers themselves came forward, and zealously united their best energies with those of the Government in making such a general and simultaneous effort as the occasion demanded. He therefore called upon every settler, whether residing

on his farm or in a town, cheerfully to render
assistance, and place himself under the direction of
the police-magistrate of his district. It was hoped
that a sufficiently numerous volunteer force would
thus be raised, which, in combination with the
whole disposable strength of the military and
police, would by one cordial and determined effort,
either capture the whole of the hostile tribes, or
permanently expel them from the settled districts.
The colonists nobly responded to the Governor's
appeal, and entered into his plans with alacrity.
His Excellency took command in person, nearly the
whole of the military were called out, the field-
police joined the line in a body, the volunteer
settlers were formed into divisions named after
their respective districts, all ticket-of-leave men
were mustered into the ranks as well as a multitude
of convicts who were either in assigned service or
otherwise at the disposal of the Government. It
will appear singular to English readers, that a body
of convicts, nearly equal in number to the military
and free volunteers, and possessing an infinitely
better acquaintance with the bush, should have
been entrusted with fire-arms by the Government—
but no wonder will be experienced by those who are

13

aware of the excellent discipline which Sir George Arthur had established among the prisoner population. Sir George's plan of campaign was to drive the blacks into the south-eastern corner of the island, every precaution being taken to prevent them breaking through the advancing line. As the divisions advanced, it was surprising, and indeed highly gratifying, to observe the good order that prevailed, and the good feeling evinced by all. Gentlemen of influence and property, youths connected with the best families in the island, marched along with the convicts, all, without exception, carrying knapsacks laden with provisions. At night large fires were constantly kept burning, and the whole country was thus illuminated in a most picturesque fashion. But unfavourable weather soon set in, and greatly impeded our operations. Nevertheless, it was ascertained that two of the tribes were encompassed, and skirmishing parties were sent out to reconnoitre. A number of blacks were encountered by one of these parties, but the opportunity of capturing them was lost, owing to the indiscretion of the skirmishers in rushing upon them, instead of quietly sending for reinforcements to thoroughly surround them. The result was that only one was captured, and the rest escaped. This unfortunate blunder proved very injurious to the success of the movement, for the aborigines now fully comprehended what we had in view, and brought all their ingenuity into play to circumvent us. Native dogs became numerous at night, a proof that the blacks were nigh, and ready to crawl through any opening in our ranks that offered a chance of escape. Subsequent accounts, derived from the blacks themselves, showed that such was really the case, and that we had, at one time, surrounded two of the most ferocious tribes. It could scarcely have been otherwise, for during the whole of this period no outrages were committed by the natives, notwithstanding that the settled districts were left practically unprotected.

The rock on which our expedition split was a dense scrub of vast extent and impervious character. It was found impossible to penetrate it and keep the line of march intact as hitherto. All our efforts to preserve the continuity of the ranks were baffled, and the aborigines were thus afforded opportunities, which they did not fail to utilise, of noiselessly gliding through the unavoidable gaps in our line. When our ranks were re-united, it was

13*

soon ascertained that the natives had broken
through the net we had been so diligently weaving
around them. The forces were dispersed, and the
movement was confessedly a costly failure. Nevertheless it had important indirect results, for the
subsequent peaceful and successful mission of Mr.
G. A. Robinson, was only made possible by our
previous demonstration of force and determination.
No conciliation was ever effected until the line had
taken the field under the command of Governor
Arthur. It was when the forces were so engaged
that Mr. Robinson scored his first success in securing
the submission of a whole tribe. I am fully
persuaded that the display of the white men's
strength and vigour frightened the blacks, and that
our march across the island contributed most to Mr.
Robinson's subsequent peaceful victory in bringing
in all the tribes. The natives themselves have
indeed since confessed that they were in a great
measure swayed by the motive I have mentioned.
They had found themselves driven from their own
hunting-grounds, forced into a corner, surrounded,
and only escaping capture after great danger and
difficulty. They imagined that we would not cease
our efforts, that we would harass them until either

surrender or extermination ensued, and they pre-
ferred the former.

Mr. G. A. Robinson, the " Apostle of the Blacks,"
was generally regarded as a madman when he
proposed nothing less than proceeding into the
wilderness with a few companions, all unarmed,
meeting the aboriginal tribes wherever practicable,
conciliating them, and persuading them to surrender themselves peaceably. But, to the astonishment
and rejoicing of the whole colony, Mr. Robinson
gradually secured the submission of the most savage
and sanguinary tribes in the island. Nothing
daunted this remarkable man. Conscious of his
philanthropic motives and of the integrity of his
intentions, he would fearlessly advance towards the
fierce and suspicious savages, extend his arms as a
sign of peace, and soon convince them that they
had nothing to fear from an unarmed party. Then
a parley would ensue, and, wonderful to relate, the
whole tribe, as if impelled by a sudden magnetic
influence, would consent to accompany Mr. Robinson
to headquarters. Mr. Robinson devoted five years
to this memorable work, and I am not aware that
he has received any very adequate remuneration for
his valuable services. I do not believe that

altogether he has received £6,000 in money and land. This is but a trifling reward in comparison to the large sums that had previously been expended on offensive and defensive operations against the blacks.

I received 100 acres of land in recognition of my services in the field, the grant being accompanied by a letter from the Colonial Secretary, intimating that if I made good use of this quantity I would be awarded an additional grant. But, with my usual imprudence, I sold the hundred acres shortly after I came into possession of them, and so forfeited the further benefits I might have enjoyed. One day, about this time, I received a note requesting me to wait on the Colonial Secretary. I did so, and some letters were handed to me, one addressed to Lord Glenelg by the Danish envoy in London, and another from his lordship to Sir George Arthur, intimating that I had succeeded to some family property in Denmark. I sent home a power of attorney and have since had from that source £200 in money, and goods to a greater amount, but as I did not make good use of this windfall, I have experienced little benefit from the accession. Throughout my life I have been exceedingly un-

fortunate in money matters. It will be remembered
that I commanded a Danish vessel of war in 1807-8
and succeeded in making several valuable captures.
My share of the prize-money amounted to a
considerable sum, but, owing to the strange course
of the events of my life, I was never in a position to
claim it.

I have now come to the conclusion of the second
part of my autobiography. It is not for me to
speculate upon whether or not I shall ever be able
to write a third instalment. This must be left to
the will of that Being who rules man's destiny.
I have had my full share of days, and little is
there in this world to care for. These pages would
have probably never appeared if I had merely
consulted my own feelings, for I am not fond of
thrusting myself on the public with unnecessary
confessions. I have been swayed by motives of a
higher character. My youthful readers may derive
a lesson from the history of my life. All human
wisdom is vanity, if not regulated by prudence.
One error leads to another, and every deviation
from the straight path is sure to lead the strayed
sheep into the mazes of a labyrinth. I will only
add that my transportation has been the means of

totally eradicating from my breast all inclination for
the horrid propensity which persecuted me for so
many years. A return to the gaming-table would
now be as severe a punishment as could well be
inflicted on me, and such is the common effect of
transportation on all prisoners in Van Diemen's
Land. The new scenes and occupations in which
they are suddenly and abruptly placed, like the
transplanting of a tree, make them pine and suffer
for a time, until restraint becomes a habit, and in
both body and mind the convict becomes a new
man. He is taught to value character as the only
means of emancipation—I mean emancipation in
the moral sense, for in Van Diemen's Land, although
a man's sentence may be completed, unless he has
cut himself free from criminal indulgences, unless
he seeks by honest industry alone to earn his
living, he is as much a convict, and even more so,
more wretched in the eyes of the surrounding
community, than if he were still in actual bondage,
a prisoner of the Crown. Placed in assigned
service, he is comparatively at large, and is in a
certain sense master of his own conduct and actions.
He is at liberty to choose his own course. Much
more dependence can be placed on the reformation

of a man so situated than upon that of a person who is never suffered to try his own depth, whose arms are, so to speak, continually tied, whose evil inclinations are in a manner kept alive by the everlasting effort to resist the restraint that is necessarily imposed upon them, and which only await its removal to burst forth in all their original wildness and wickedness. Prisons, hulks, and penitentiaries, generally speaking, rear a race of hypocrites and sycophants. Whilst they seem to repress, they accumulate and intensify the disposition to the very worst of crimes. Thus convicts, on being set at large in England, immediately resort to their former acquaintances, and recommence their former depredations on society. There is a species of madness and delusion hanging over the minds of persons addicted to crime which can only be cured by change of scene—the absence and the treatment which transportation only can secure.

Casting a retrospective glance on the picture I have drawn of myself, I feel that candour has induced me to paint it occasionally in less favourable colours than those employed by the learned Dr. Hooker, or the biographer in the preface to my theological work. But my business was not to palliate, but to expose, the great error of my life, so that, as I conceive, a moral lesson may be derived from it. I remember a Quaker at Whitby, who once delivered a very impressive discourse from the eccentric text : "Every tub shall stand upon its own bottom and every herring hang by its own tail." Similarly, the success or failure of the foregoing narrative must rest entirely upon its own merits or imperfections.

APPENDIX A.

JORGENSON, throughout all his vicissitudes of fortune, was an industrious and voluminous writer, but com- paratively few of the products of his pen are accessible now-a-days. His first published volume was a con- tribution to current religious controversy under the title of " The State of Christianity in the Island of Otaheite." The author made his purpose plain on the title-page by describing his book as " A defence of the pure precepts of the gospel against modern anti-Christs, with reasons for the ill success which attends Christian missionaries in their attempts to

convert the heathens." It was published in a large
volume of 175 pages by J. Hatchard, Piccadilly, and
dedicated in a characteristically effusive epistle to
John Berkeley Monk, "the generous descendant
of the illustrious and loyal Albemarle," in whose
house, Jorgenson says, he received the sincerest
welcome and the noblest hospitality. He strikes
the key-note of his attack with the declaration that
" the contemplating mind is lost in amazement on
perceiving a religion, which teaches nothing but
charity and fraternal love, meet with so much
opposition as it generally does, where it is attempted
to be introduced." He attributes this opposition to
two principal causes :—(1.) The ignorance, bigotry,
violence and indecent behaviour of those men, called
missionaries, sent abroad for the purpose of propa-
gating Christianity, and (2.) The manner in which
preachers of the Gospel attempt to convert the
heathens and others, which tends rather to perplex
their minds, and give them a contemptible idea, not
only of missionaries, but even of religion itself, than
to enlighten the natives. He then proceeds to
address himself at considerable length to the proof
of these two assertions, by giving the results of his
observations on the work of the missionaries during

his stay on the island of Otaheite, which he
mentions in an early portion of his autobiography.
The picture he gives of the missionaries of his day
is lurid and unflattering in the extreme. But there
are also passages in the book exhibiting no little
shrewdness and insight into native character. Here
for instance is some excellent advice, not unworthy
of attention by all engaged in missionary enterprise
at the present time :

"If men who settle among the heathens for the
purpose of introducing Christianity would, in the
first instance, not open their lips at all about the
superior merit of our religion, or depreciate that of
the country in which they reside, they would find
much less opposition. Let them begin with
showing the natives all the good-nature and friendship they can, let them endeavour to instruct the
natives in useful arts and social duties, and
let them demean themselves in such a manner
that the pagan will fall in love with the man
and his virtues before he is taught by word of
mouth the precepts of Christianity. The heathen
will listen with peculiar pleasure to one whom he
esteems and reverences, and will wish to imitate his

upright and disinterested conduct. He will be a
practical Christian before he knows the name of
Christ, and he will glory in being the follower of
One who has done so much good to mankind."

Jorgenson's "Travels through France and
Germany"—a bulky volume of 432 pages issued by
Cadell & Davies, Strand—was honoured by an
extended notice of twenty pages in the *Edinburgh
Review*, on its first publication. The reason assigned
for this special distinction was "the peculiarity of
the journey described in this volume having been
performed on foot."

" It was," says the reviewer, "the expectation of
receiving facts, the result of actual observation
respecting the country and the people, collected in
an intercourse with them much more close than
almost any other traveller has had, that induced us
to go through Mr. Jorgenson's book with care."

In this expectation the reviewer confesses that he
was somewhat disappointed, that Jorgenson had
given more dissertations than facts. And this was
undoubtedly an accurate estimate of the book.
Jorgenson was evidently of opinion that the time
had not yet come for a full statement of the facts

attending his confidential mission to the Continent.
Twenty years afterwards, when he was writing his
autobiography in Van Diemen's Land, he committed
to paper some of the information which the
Edinburgh Review not unreasonably expected to
find in the first published account of his travels.

As he arrived on the Continent just in time to
witness the final and irrevocable overthrow of
Napoleon at Waterloo, Jorgenson could not resist
the temptation of embodying in his record of travel
a lengthy review of the character and conduct of the
fallen Cæsar. He sums Napoleon up as a great
military commander, who fell into the same error
which had proved fatal to so many other conquerors
—that of teaching the art of war to their enemies,
and then of disregarding them. Jorgenson entered
Paris at a time when " it contained within its walls
the greatest sovereigns of Europe, the most
illustrious commanders, the most able and most distinguished diplomatists. The gay, the curious, the
witty, the learned, the fool that had more money than
wit, the knave who possessed more of the latter than
the former—all had flocked to Paris, some to ruin
themselves, and some to raise their fortunes." He
adds that " the little bonnet and the neat modest

habit of an Englishwoman excited much ridicule
amongst the Parisians. During my stay in the
city there were several English ladies of the
highest rank, who obstinately adhered to their own
country customs and who were greatly admired
by some foreign sovereigns and princes, but the
French declared that they had no taste and looked
like monsters. The French fashion about this
time was to wear a very lofty bonnet, resembling
in miniature the tower on the back of an
elephant. A head furniture of this kind, about
14 inches in height, had the effect of making the
French women look somewhat dwarfish, and from
a very natural reason. The body of a person
appears longer or shorter in proportion to the
dimensions of the head ; now if the latter be extended by artificial means to a great length, the
former will seem more contracted than it really is."

An inveterate gambler like Jorgenson, it is needless to remark after what he has himself told us in
his autobiography, could not resist the fascinations
of the Parisian gaming-houses, and he devotes a
whole chapter to his experiences and observations
within these dangerous establishments. "The con-
course of people," he says, " who flock to these sinks

of iniquity, is far beyond description. During the
time I was at Paris an amazing number of foreign
officers resorted thither to ruin themselves. One
day I saw a military gentleman of considerable rank,
who, after losing a large sum of money, took three
different decorations of honour which were fastened
to the button-holes of his coat, and sold them for a
trifle to a bystander. Having staked the whole of
the money thus obtained on a colour and lost, he
rushed out of the room with every symptom of
despair." After narrating several other incidents of
the like character that came under his notice in the
Parisian gaming - houses, Jorgenson proceeds to
philosophise on the evil in a strain that is singularly daring, considering what a slave to this
particular vice he was himself. " Why men with
their eyes open should thus rush into certain
destruction, after the repeated defeats of their
hopes have shown the folly of their perseverance,
is a question by no means easy of solution. In
every game of hazard the advantage is so greatly on
the side of the bank that it cannot escape the notice
even of the most common understanding. In no
other case would a man enter on the transaction of
business with the odds so clearly against him ; yet

14

here we see him place the utmost confidence in the flattering aspect of fortune."

Our author professes to have found little to admire in the France he saw at the close of the Hundred Days. He says he entered the country with the most favourable prepossessions, but, with the exception of a comparatively few individuals, he came across little that corresponded with the flattering opinion he had formed of the French nation. On the other hand he discovered many excellent qualities, concealed under an apparently rough exterior, amongst the Germans, whom he describes as free from guile, honest and upright, ever ready to render a real service when in their power—in short, a patriotic, brave, and loyal nation. " I quit Germany," he says, " with feelings of gratitude more easily conceived than described.   Nowhere (and I have been a sojourner in many countries) have I found more sincerity of heart, more frankness of manners, more good-will towards their fellow-men, than in the brave and honest German nation."

" The Religion of Christ the Religion of Nature ', is the book that Jorgenson wrote in Newgate, and to which, he says, he devoted no small amount of study and attention. According to the author's account it was published outside without his knowledge, and made him so many enemies in influential quarters that the authorities were induced to order his transportation to Van Diemen's Land—a course that they did not originally contemplate. It was issued in a large volume of 429 pages by Joseph Capes, Fleet Street, with a biographical preface by " H. D. M.," who does not explain how the manuscript of the book came into his possession, but contents himself with briefly summarising in a few pages Jorgenson's stirring career up to date. What there was in the book to give offence in high places, and to bring about the banishment of its author, is not easy to discover at this time of day. English unbelievers of a couple of generations ago must have been peculiarly sensitive if they lost their tempers over a not particularly well-ordered compilation of all the evidences of Christianity that could be collected within the limited confines of Newgate. No doubt Jorgenson's language is somewhat vehement at times, and the tone of the book throughout is ultra - controversial. He announces his purpose at the start in this uncompromising fashion :

"When I observe doctrines promulgated so
repugnant to the best feelings of the human
mind, and so diametrically at variance with the
Holy Scriptures and right reason, I cannot refrain
from doing all in my power, not only to expose the
idle and indefinite jargon of the philosophers, but
to show that the Religion of Christ is the Religion
of Nature."

He then sets about marshalling all the arguments against atheism that he can command, and
incidentally makes the following profession of
faith :—

"I, for my part, place the most implicit belief
in the account given in the Scriptures of the ante-
diluvian world, because I defy any human art,
contrivance or ingenuity to produce a similar
account so self-evident, so clear and concise. The
Bible preserves an undeviating consistency in all its
parts and relations, never stating any fact where the
human reason cannot trace a just necessity. The
entire account is agreeable to the nature of man
and the nature of things. No one has as yet, with
authority or without authority, supplied mankind

with even a rational conjecture of the origin of all things, except what we learn from the Scriptures. The writers could never have been actuated by corrupt motives or an intention to impose on mankind. Their aim was clearly to promote virtue and hold up vice to detestation, objects connected with the happiness of all human beings. The subjects recorded have a visible connection with the other parts of the Scriptures subsequently written, making the whole a work of uniformity, directly bearing upon the grand design of our Creator."

Towards the close of the book, the imprisoned author permits himself to indulge in a rhapsodical flight that is in curious contrast to the ignoble circumstances of his present, and the grievous uncertainty of his future.

"Should those be in the right," he exclaims, "who consign man to die the death of a beast of the field, to be for ever annihilated and confounded with the grossest matter, then would my days be days of misery, despair would mark my footsteps, profound grief and melancholy would seize upon my soul, the hours of night would be the constant witnesses of my tears, I should have to relinquish all those flattering ideas and fond hopes which have rendered my peregrination through life tolerable to me. From my earliest youth I have been taught to look up to my Creator as one most holy, most wise, and most good, but now neither the glories of the sun, the pale beauties of the moon, nor the pleasant sight of the fields could for one moment dispel the cloud of doubt hanging over my mind: all, all within me would be dismay and confusion. I could scarcely help questioning the Divine wisdom and goodness. As a human creature I enjoy the powers of contemplation, yet I should never be able to discern any wise design in the creation. Generation after generation follow each other in rapid succession, and to me it would appear as for no other visible purpose than to look about them for a few moments, then drop into the grave, and the grosser elements of nature would reign lords paramount of the creation. Every honourable and, virtuous feeling of my mind would be outraged; were it in my power I would change myself into a block of stone without sense or motion; I should envy the lot of the reptile creeping on the earth."

The amateur theologian and professional adventurer gives his Christian reader some valedictory advice, that reads like the peroration of a sermon by some Evangelical divine : — " If in the midst of temptation you preserve your faith pure and perfect ; if in prosperity moderate, and in adversity patient ; if you act with charity towards your brother, if you rely on the promises of your Saviour, if you truly repent of your sins—then, most assuredly, you will in due time obtain that high reward which God has decreed to righteousness. You shall partake of the glories of His Kingdom, and your felicity shall be never-ceasing."

The *Gentleman's Magazine* accorded this book of Jorgenson's an extended and appreciative notice :— " We are prepared," it says, " to speak of this volume in high terms, and yet we consider it rather as curious than valuable. It is curious as coming from one who will possess a niche in history, as displaying considerable acuteness, as having been written in a peculiar situation, and from its scientific character ; but its value is lessened (paradoxical as the remark may seem) by some of these very causes, for the leisure of a prison is not like that of the closet, neither can the literary attainments of a potentate or of a felon (for such the author alternately was) equal those of a student. With this and some other considerations, to be mentioned afterwards, we enter upon the examination of a work whose title creates an interest which is not lessened by a perusal of its contents." In the course of this detailed examination, the *Gentleman's* reviewer awards high honours to Jorgenson as a controversialist. " He possesses the rare talent of setting two infidel theories against each other, and carrying the argument away from them both; sometimes he plays with his adversary, as a cat with a mouse, gives him liberty to range for a while, then contracts his space, and at last crushes him with a grasp."

The *Gentleman's* reviewer finally sums up the book as " a valuable addition to our stores of natural theology. The style is often ironical, sometimes foreign in its idioms, and occasionally ungrammatical to our ears. We conclude with sincerest wishes that the author may live to show himself worthy of the dignified position he once held, as well as of the happy mind to which he is now brought. The literary labours of historical personages are always interesting, even if less intrinsically valuable than this volume; nor can we imagine a fairer likelihood of fame than his whose political career will be perpetuated in the annals of his country, whose conversion will secure to him a prominent post in those of religion, and whose arguments will be cited as conclusive in the most important of controversies."

From the lofty and edifying moral teaching of Jorgenson's *magnum opus*, it is a somewhat abrupt and, possibly, profane descent to the same pious gentleman's " Observations on the Funded System : A Summary View of the Present Political State of Great Britain and the Relative Situation in which the Colony of Van Diemen's Land stands towards the Mother Country." This is a reprint of a series of articles contributed by Jorgenson to the *Colonial Times*, published in a volume of 134 pages, by H. Melville, Hobart. The economic theory, which the ex-King of Iceland elaborates in this treatise, is, that English pauperism, and all its attendant evils, are directly traceable to the funded system, which, he alleges, has created a mischievous aristocracy of wealth and usury. Its baneful effects extend even to the remote Antipodes. " A gentleman asked me, a few days ago, ' what concern have we in Van Diemen's

Land with the funded system of England ? ' I
answer, that the funded system of the United
Kingdom exerts an influence over the pecuniary
transactions of the whole civilised world. I further
say that, had Britain not been involved in debt, the
British Government would not have been guilty of
the excessive meanness and injustice of depriving
this infant colony of such a paltry sum as £30,000,
which had been laid by for the construction of
roads and bridges, and for providing against other
exigencies that are likely to arise in a new and
undeveloped country."

Into Jorgenson's proposals for the extinction of
the National Debt, it is unnecessary to enter, but
the opinion he had formed of the land of his exile,
when the evening of his adventurous life was approaching, may be worth noting.

Having, he says, for upwards of thirty-five years
travelled in many parts of the globe, and looked at
everything with a scrutinising eye, he knew of no
country where man could live so happily as Van
Diemen's Land, if only the British Government
would leave the administration of local matters to
those who understand them. With the cessation of
such undue interference, at the hands of far-away

and ill-informed officials, the Colony would thrive
and prosper beyond any other dependency of the
Crown.

It is only within a comparatively recent period
that Downing Street has learnt the lesson here
indicated, wisely decided to loosen the reins, and
advantageously allowed the Colonies to work out
their own destiny with native vigour and enterprise.

APPENDIX B.

OF Jorgenson's unpublished writings, there are five large volumes in the Egerton collection of manuscripts in the British Museum. The first, and the most ambitious, fills 517 closely-written pages, and was composed during the author's detention in Tothill Fields prison, after his brief and merry career as a monarch in Iceland. It is entitled "The Adventures of Thomas Walter," and is dedicated in a prefatory letter to Sir William Hooker, whom Jorgenson describes as " the only one who has had sufficient courage to address me as ' My Dear Friend.'" This book is a curious and entertaining

mixture of fact and fiction. On the basis of his
extensive experience as a traveller in many lands,
and a voyager over many seas, Jorgenson has built
up a succession of imaginary adventures, evidently
in imitation of the manner of Swift and Defoe,
some of his stories being tender and pathetic,
whilst others are characterised by a coarse, riotous
and Rabelaisian style of humour. As an English
composition it is far from faultless, but this is not
surprising in view of the circumstances under which
it was written. "The prisoners are generally either
swearing, cursing or fiddling," says Jorgenson in his
preface, " and every moment I am in dread of somebody or other tumbling over me and spoiling all I
have written." England is described in the book
under the disguise of Capricornia, and London as
Thamas, France figures as Badocia, Denmark as
Odinia, and Germany as Almadia. No small
portion of the volume is occupied by reflections
on the manners, customs, and characteristic
qualities of the peoples of these countries.
For instance, "It is not from external foes the
Capricornians have anything to fear. Their navy,
their valour, their courage, their love for their
country, will always prevent an evil of that kind.

To suppose Capricornia can be invaded is
perfectly ridiculous to every man of common
sense, but this great, this glorious nation, has addicted itself so much to luxury and extravagance
within recent years that I foresee innumerable evils
which may undermine its happiness and plunge
Capricornia into many dangers and difficulties.   If
being oppressed by one tyrant is an evil, to be the
slaves of luxury is a greater evil still.   Should the
Capricornians ever be conquered, it must be by
themselves, they will never be conquered by
others."

This manuscript volume is illustrated with
several pictures in black and white, drawn by
Jorgenson to beguile the tedium of prison life.
One exhibits an amusing incident at an Iceland
ball, another shows us the hulk *Bahama*, in which
Jorgenson was confined, with a view of the Chatham
of the period in the background, and a third
portrays Jorgenson's early friend and patron, Sir
Joseph Banks, as a Mæcenas rescuing the arts and
sciences driven from the Continent by revolutionary
violence.   Two of them are pictorial allegories,
into which he has introduced his own portrait,
first as a captive and afterwards as a free man.

"JORGENSON FREE."

(From the original drawing by J. Jorgenson, in the Egerton Collection at the British Museum.)

They are intended to illustrate a dream of the ex-
king, in which he beheld himself sitting desolate and
in irons before an altar on which an aged priest was
sacrificing to Tyranny and Oppression. The Goddess
of Liberty appears, but is unable to approach the
captive, whereupon she ascends to Olympus and
invokes the aid of mighty Jove, who arms her
with a thunderbolt, with which she strikes and
shivers into fragments the altar of Tyranny and
releases the captive king. These pictures were
obviously planned and designed by Jorgenson to
stimulate Sir William Hooker and other influential
friends of his to redouble their exertions to obtain
his release from Tothill Fields prison, where he was
confined at the time in consequence of his Icelandic
escapade.

" The Kingdom of Shandaria and the Adventures
of King Detrimedes," is projected on somewhat
similar lines to the preceding. It is also dedicated
to Sir William Hooker, and bears the motto, " I
was in prison and ye came unto me." It fills
433 pages. As may be guessed from the title, it
belongs to a class of writings now familiar to the
reading world, the numerous progeny of Sir
Thomas More's " Utopia," the host of books in

which imaginary kingdoms are founded, and ideal
civilisations built up to the perfect satisfaction of
the self-complacent author. Jorgenson's mythical
kingdom is vaguely described as situated in Asia,
beyond the dominions of the Great Mogul. According to the maps, its site is occupied by a vast
desert, peopled only by a few nomadic tribes, but,
according to Jorgenson, it is in reality one of the
finest countries in the world, inhabited by a race
whose manners, customs, religion, government and
laws are worthy of the most serious study and the
heartiest admiration. Shandaria is exhibited as
showing all the advantages to be derived from a
benevolent despotism—no poverty, no insanity, no
prisons, no drunkenness, no lawyers, no doctors, no
communication with foreigners, none of the evils, in
short, that afflict society as constituted in real
matter-of-fact monarchies. It is not surprising
that Jorgenson should express himself very feelingly
on the subject of the total absence of prisons in his
mythical kingdom, for whilst his imagination was
thus roaming at large, his body was confined within
the limits of a Westminster prison as a punishment
for the little unauthorised experiment in benevolent
despotism that he himself had initiated in Iceland.

" In the kingdom of Shandaria," he says, " there
are never seen loathsome gaols, places of confinement, bolts, irons, and other such disgraceful
implements and witnesses of human folly." A
considerable portion of the book is devoted to a
protracted discussion with the mythical King of
Shandaria on the merits of the Christian religion.

Jorgenson's " Historical Account of a Revolution
in Iceland, in the year 1809," is a detailed narrative
of his deposition of Count Tramp and his assumption
of the sovereignty, supplemented by a vindication
of his conduct throughout the whole extraordinary
affair.   It fills 381 pages, and, with characteristic
audacity is dedicated without permission to the
" Most Noble the Marquis of Wellesley, Minister
for Foreign Affairs in the United Kingdom of
Great Britain and Ireland."   The facts as set forth
in this unpublished manuscript are substantially
the same as he subsequently recorded in his now-
published autobiography written in Van Diemen's
Land, the only difference being that the former
bears abundant evidence of the natural heat and
excitement under which he laboured immediately
after the occurrence of the events described,
whereas the latter, composed thirty years after-

wards in exile, states the circumstances with more of the sobriety, calmness and moderation of an old man looking back, in the evening of life, upon the various incidents of a stormy and adventurous career.

Here is one highly rhetorical passage from Jorgenson's manuscript vindication of his conduct as King of Iceland. "If there are any charges against me, let the people making them come forward in an open, fair and candid manner; let me see the accusers face to face, and how easily shall I confront them! But this they dread, for the truth must prevail. Where in the name of God is there any man in Iceland that can make a just complaint against me? Is anyone injured in property or liberty? Is there any innocent blood crying for vengeance against me? If I have shed the blood of a fellow creature in Iceland, either justly or unjustly, let my head pay for it! If I have enriched myself to the detriment of a single individual, let my left hand be cut off! If I have caused a single person to be confined for being opposed in principles to me, let me be consigned to all the horrors of perpetual imprisonment! But, if I have done none of these things, let me enjoy that liberty which I look upon as the only true good on earth. If the British Government has a power to crush, it has also the power to be merciful, and if ever a man deserved generous treatment from that government it is I, for I have sacrificed all my worldly prospects rather than serve against Great Britain."

Two of Jorgenson's plays are preserved in manuscript in the British Museum—the five-act tragedy entitled "The Duc D'Enghien" to which he incidentally refers in his autobiography, and a satirical piece, also in five acts, styled "Robertus Montanus; or The Oxford Scholar." He is more successful in the second than the first. The tragedy opens with a scene somewhat reminiscent of "Hamlet," the ghost of Henry IV. appearing as the genius of France to the young Bourbon Prince and commanding him to arise and deliver his country from the tyranny of the Corsican usurper. He promises to obey the behest of his illustrious ancestor, enters into a conspiracy with General Moreau for the destruction of Bonaparte, and the restoration of the Bourbons, but the designs of the conspirators are betrayed to the Emperor by a soldier who accidentally overhears their conversation. The Duke is seized, brought before Bonaparte,

and the most dramatic scene of the play is then
enacted, the princely prisoner declaiming a lurid
impeachment of the military autocrat, who at length
starts up in ungovernable rage, orders his accuser
out of his presence and resolves on the Duke's
immediate condemnation to death. The Bourbon
Princess Adelaide and the Empress Josephine supply
the feminine interest of the drama.

"Robertus Montanus; or The Oxford Scholar"
may be classed amongst what are known now-a-days
as farcical comedies. The hero, Robert Hill, is the
son of honest but unlearned parents in an English
village, who spend their little all in giving him an
Oxford education. He returns to the village full
of academic lore, and causes consternation amongst
the simple-minded folks by upsetting all their time-
honoured notions and beliefs. He alienates his
intended father-in-law by asserting and maintaining
the novel and highly-objectionable doctrine that
the earth is round, not flat, as all the villagers
had hitherto supposed from the evidence of their
senses. At length after having plunged the little
community into all sorts of dissensions, and converted
a peaceful village into a sort of miniature pande-
monium, the pedantic arch-disturber is cleverly

caught by a recruiting lieutenant, who subjects him
to a severe course of discipline and speedily subdues
his intellectual pride. The last act shows him
thoroughly tamed and listening in all humility
to such friendly advice as this :

"Endeavour to get out of your head what you have
spent so much time in putting into it, and employ
your time for the future in something useful."

The idea of the piece is carefully and creditably
worked out, and the result is a far more satisfactory
piece of dramatic work than the ambitious tragedy
founded on the violent end of the ill-fated Prince of
the House of Bourbon.

Jorgenson was a most industrious and painstaking
correspondent, and his numerous letters to Sir
William Hooker, Mr. Dawson Turner, and Mr.
Henry Jermyn, form the fifth and final volume of his
manuscript works in the British Museum. They
are a mirror of his Micawber-like character, exhibiting
him one day soaring high on the pinions of hope,
and on the next plunged in the lowest depths of
despair. Most of them were written from the inside
of London prisons; a few were dated from the
respectable and refined quarter of Tavistock Place;
others issued from a sponging-house in the neigh

bourhood of Lincoln's Inn Fields, of which he gives a very graphic description, and several were sent from his retreat at Reading, during one of the brief intervals of comparative calm in his tempestuous career in the northern hemisphere.

It would seem that during his detention in New-gate, Jorgenson officiated not only as hospital assistant, but also as occasional preacher to the prisoners. He makes no mention of the fact in his autobiography, but what purports to be a selection from his sermons in Newgate is bound up with his correspondence in the British Museum. These sermons are certainly in his handwriting, but whether they are genuine and original compositions of his is a question that cannot so easily be deter-mined. They have undoubtedly a sort of Jorgen-sonian ring and a courageous audacity about them that would seem to point to the ex-king of Iceland as their probable author. This is the exordium of the first of these singular exhortations :

" There is something extremely affecting to the mind in the idea of having known a person in the full vigour of manhood who is suddenly called away by the Lord. Some of you I have seen and conversed with; therefore it is my most anxious wish to afford you all the aid and consolation in my power, that you may appear before your Heavenly Judge without fear and trembling. The fate of some of you in this world is, I am sorely afraid, irrevocably sealed, and thus the few moments you have yet to linger in this vale of grief and sorrow should unceasingly be fixed on the salvation of your souls. My present discourse will be limited to two objects of vast importance: to strengthen your faith and to show you what sort of repentance can only be acceptable to God."

An extract from another Jorgensonian sermon may be given, in which shrewd worldly wisdom is deftly interwoven with higher religious considerations:

"I still entertain such regard for humanity that I think no man would become vicious but for a mistaken notion that vice produces happiness. Let us examine this matter thoroughly. The old proverb most assuredly holds good, that 'honesty is the best policy.' Look around you, and see what you have gained by your vicious pursuits. The man whom you laughed at and ridiculed, whom you called a fool, whom you defrauded, walks erect on the face of the earth without fear or reproach, whilst you are shackled with irons, and have to endure all sorts of suffering and degradation. Who now is the wisest man? Where are those faithless friends that shared in your ill-gotten booty? They have deserted you in the hour of tribulation. Observe the difference when a truly honest man is in distress or when he is unjustly accused. Kind friends and neighbours will administer consolation; they will sympathise with his sorrows, and exert all the influence in their power to rescue him from impending danger."

The other writings of Jorgenson have apparently perished. His treatise on "The Copenhagen Expedition" is not accessible now, although it is referred to in one of his letters as having been printed and published. The same observation applies to his "Statistical Account of the Russian Empire." Jorgenson's "History of the Black War in Van Diemen's Land,"—a movement in which he bore an active and prominent part—was presented in manuscript to Archdeacon Braim, of Portland,

Victoria, who placed it at the disposal of Mr. James Bonwick, when that industrious investigator into the colonial events of the past was compiling his interesting work on "The Lost Tasmanian Race." Portions of Jorgenson's narrative are quoted in Mr. Bonwick's book.

In closing the record of the unique career of this audacious and versatile adventurer, the question naturally suggests itself—Was Jorgenson entirely sane? It is evident that in the many strange and startling vicissitudes that make up the bustling story of his life, he was more frequently and more powerfully swayed by momentary impulse than by the dictates of reason. He has anticipated a controversy that is current at the present time, as to whether genius is allied to insanity, and, with this psychological study of himself, the curtain may appropriately descend on the stirring drama of "The Convict King." Writing from 1, Duke's Row, Tavistock Place, to Sir William Hooker, on his return from his Continental tour as a confidential agent of the British Foreign Office, Jorgenson says, "I have thousands of things to tell you—wonders indeed—and when I reveal to you my adventures within these last four years,

16

they will have more the appearance of romance
than reality. During my late peregrinations I have
succeeded in attracting the notice of some of the
highest and most powerful characters on the Continent, who are as willing as they are able to use
their interest and influence on my behalf. Yet,
strange as it may appear, there are some curious
peculiarities attached to my character, which baffle
the penetration of my best friends and well-wishers,
and which puzzle my own mind to such a degree at
times that, even in my most solitary hours and in
the midst of deepest meditation, I cannot understand myself. These peculiarities have sometimes
been considered in a strong light, and have
rendered my friends suspicious of my reason. Yet
after taking a careful and repeated survey of my
own mind, I think genius may often be mistaken
for madness. My good-natured friend, do not smile
at my presumption. I talk to myself when I talk
to you. . . . . But now I am convinced that
the greatest human happiness consists in the attain-
ment of a certain equanimity, which is much more
suitable to our natures than wild schemes of ambition or worldly advantages. The highest privileges
of the mind, if not rightly applied to some great

purpose, are of little avail, and the most splendid situations of life are as nought in comparison with that happy tranquillity where science is the companion of virtue."

THE END.

For EU product safety concerns, contact us at Calle de José Abascal, 56–1°, 28003 Madrid, Spain or eugpsr@cambridge.org.

www.ingramcontent.com/pod-product-compliance
Ingram Content Group UK Ltd.
Pitfield, Milton Keynes, MK11 3LW, UK
UKHW010342140625
459647UK00010B/767